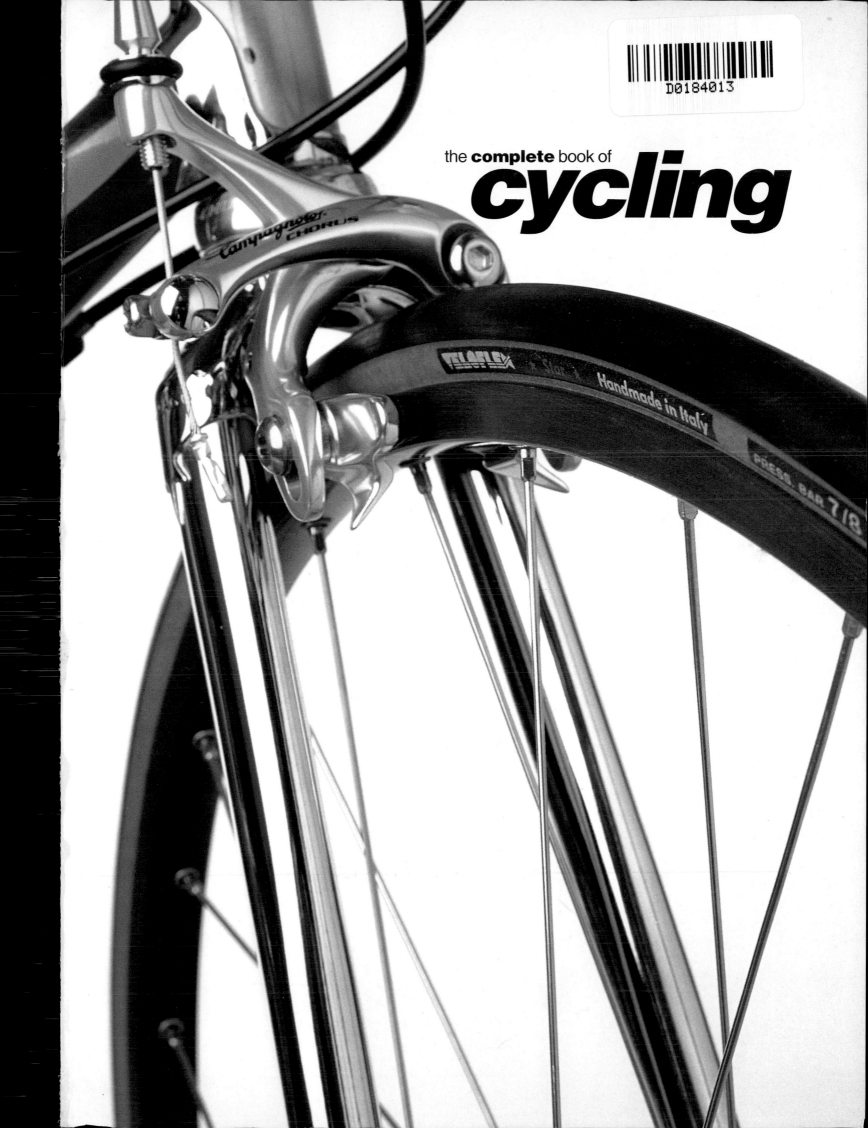

the **complete** book of
cycling

the **complete** book of
cycling

Dan **Joyce**
Carlton **Reid**
Paul **Vincent**

Commissioned photography
Tim **Woodcock**

CHANCELLOR
PRESS

CONTENTS

Acknowledgements

Cover and Design: Darren Kirk
Design Manager: Bryan Dunn
Art Director: Keith Martin
Picture research: Jenny Faithful
Production: Mark Walker
Publishing Director: Laura Bamford
Editor: Adam Ward
Commissioned photography: Tim Woodcock

Photographer's note
Many thanks to the following people for supplying
equipment for the photoshoot:
Ampro (WTB); Audax UK; Avocet Computers; Caratti
Sport Ltd (GT, Shogun, Rock Shox, Lake, Kirtland,
Vetta, Cyclops, Qranc, Tioga, Kryptonite, Camelbak);
Fisher Outdoor Leisure; Geoff Apps (Litage); High-5
Nutrition; Hope Technology; Ison Distribution; Leisure
Systems International (Polar); Madison Cycles plc
(Shimano, Gary Fisher, Blackburn, Finish Line, Park,
VistaLite, Gyro, Profile); Mavic; Michelin Tyres plc;
Middleburn; Oakley plc; Pashley Cycles plc; Polaris
Apparelle; Ralph Coleman Cycles, Taunton,
Somerset; Sachs; Schwalbe Tyres; Silva (UK) Ltd;
Terra Nova Equipment Ltd; Timax Ti Cycles; Venhill
Engineering (Magura); Windwave (Marzocchi, Club
Roost); X-Lite Ltd; Yellow (Nalini, Castelli); Yeovil
Cycle Centre, Yeovil, Somerset; Zoobits Ltd (Swiss
DT), Zyro plc (Cateye, Panaracer, Minoura, Viscount).

Editor's note
The editor would like to thank Rab MacWilliam, Peter
Arnold, David Ballheimer and Sarah Ford for their
help on this project.

Imperial or metric?
In the British bike world, which is what all three
authors deal in, both imperial and metric measurements are regularly used. Some things are only
measured in inches, some in centimetres, some
either. It's just the way it is. For reference, 1 inch =
2.54 centimetres.

Credit where credit's due
Dan says he wouldn't have been able to write the sections
on training to race, training for children, or nutrition without
learning from a number of excellent articles supplied to
Cycling Plus by Richard Davison and Janet Pidcock.

First published in Great Britain in 1997 by Hamlyn.
This edition published in 2000 by Chancellor Press,
an imprint of Bounty Books, a division of the
Octopus Publishing Group Ltd,
2–4 Heron Quays, London, E14 4JP

Copyright © 1997 Octopus Publishing Group Ltd

ISBN 0 75370 282 7

A CIP catalogue record for this book is available from
the British Library

Produced by Toppan (HK) Ltd
Printed in China

GET RIDING

This book shows you how to get more out of your cycling. It shows you how to buy a bike that suits *you*. It shows you how to ride it, whether you're going across town or across Africa, whether you're scorching down the road, racing against the clock, or dodging rocks on a mountain bike race circuit. It shows you how cycling can make you healthy. And it shows you how you can keep your bike healthy too.

This book certainly isn't an owner's manual. Owner's manuals are the grease for complicated machines, like cars or computers, brought out in desperation when things start to seize. Cycling is simpler than that. Bikes use technology that everyone can – in all senses of the word – grasp.

So why buy a book on something this simple? Because in an age where cheap bikes are the norm it's far too easy to get it wrong; the wrong bike, like a pair of shoes two sizes too small, is a complete misery. A bike that's badly maintained is dangerous. A cyclist who doesn't know how to ride his bike properly is an accident waiting to happen. And, on a positive note, because the scope of cycling isn't immediately obvious.

For too long the bike has been portrayed as a toy, or as sports equipment for the fitness fanatic. It can be these things, but it's more besides. A bike can get you to work cheaper and faster than a car or bus. A bike can carry a

The appearance of the 'go anywhere, do anything' mountain bike in the '80s caused a huge resurgence in cycling.

Most bicycle maintenance is very easy and cheap to perform.

substantial load – either in panniers or a trailer. A bike can turn a trudging Sunday walk into a breeze. A bike lets you race under your own power at speeds only race horses can match. A bike will take you to anywhere on earth – from the Dead Sea to the top of Mount Kilimanjaro – or all the way around it.

Cycling isn't easy to pigeonhole. A bike is a tool that can be used and enjoyed in many different ways. What might start as a hobby – the odd weekend ride, a puncture mended, a local race entered – may soon become a way of life. That's why you need this book.

Above: Riding a bike is good for your health, good for the environment and – more importantly – good for the soul: it's fun.

THE RIGHT BIKE

*'When I see an adult on a bicycle,
I have hope for the human race.'* **H.G. Wells**

Anyone who has breezed along a country lane in summer, through hedgerow scents and bird song, knows this simple truth: cycling is its own justification. It's *fun*. Children learn this as soon as they start riding; adults often forget.

The car is king for those old enough to drive. Many people will happily drive across a congested town to sweat for half an hour in a gym on a static exercise bike. Crazy. Many more won't do even that. Maybe it's because – as various health correspondents claim – we really are becoming couch potatoes. But part of the problem no doubt comes from a wrong-headed idea that cycling is dangerous, expensive, and hard work.

Cycling is safe

Back in the 1870s when men with walrus moustaches rode Ordinary bicycles (Penny Farthings), cycling was a risky business. The slightest irregularity in the road could cause a headlong dive from the shoulder-high saddle. Such dives, or 'headers', could be fatal.

The modern bike is a completely different beast altogether. The chain drive to the rear wheel gives you a less precipitous centre of gravity – this style of bike was therefore called 'the safety bike' way back in the 1880s when it was invented – and modern bicycle brakes actually work.

True, cyclists today have motorised traffic to contend with, and lots of it, but the British Medical Association reckons you're a lot more likely to die of a heart attack from a sedentary lifestyle if you *don't* cycle than you are to get hit by a bus if you *do*.[1]

With the right skills, equipment and attitude, you can minimize road dangers; more on this in the next chapter. But if you want to keep away from cars, you can. Get a mountain bike and head for the nearest bridleway. Or try to use a cycle path when possible.

Cycling is cheap

Once upon a time a bike would cost a working man three month's wages. No longer. Now little more than a week's wages – £300 – will buy you a satisfactory starter bike. If even this sounds a lot, consider that the running costs are virtually nil. And the bike could easily last a lifetime.

Perhaps because of these low prices, bikes are selling well. Since the mountain bike boom of the '80s, around two million bikes have been sold in Britain each year. Yet few of these – about one in five – are used regularly.

Typically, the owners of the other four out of five find cycling uncomfortable or hard work. Sometimes it's the fault of a bike that's just too cheap. You cannot get a decent adult's bike for £99 new. You may have fun on it a few times, but the fun, like the bike, will not last.

Opposite page: 'Penny Farthings' had a precipitous centre of gravity and one useless brake. Crashes were common. The modern bike is a much safer beast.

Quick fact

'Cycling is one of the simplest and most effective ways of getting fit,' according to the British Medical Association, which has called on the Government to improve public health by getting more people to cycle[1]. Most of us (90% of men and 67% of women[2]) can cycle, and yet around three quarters of the adult population (72% of men and 87% of women[3]) are below their appropriate fitness levels.

1. Cycling Towards Health & Safety, 1992, Oxford University Press.
2. On Your Bike: Cycling Patterns, Benefits, Constraints and Recommendations, I Sharpe, 1990. (A briefing paper for the National Forum for Coronary Heart Disease Prevention, London.)
3. Allied Dunbar National Fitness Survey, Sports Council and Health Education Authority, 1992.

Left: Compared to running, riding a road bike feels like man-powered flight. You get back so much speed for so little effort.

Below: Bikes move at just the right speed – fast enough to go somewhere, slow enough to see everything.

Cycling is easy

Cycling is the most energy efficient form of muscle powered locomotion on the planet – as long as you do it right. For one thing, the bike must be properly maintained (see Maintenance section, page 104). A rusted chain or soft tyres make cycling hard work.

The bike must also be the correct size for you. Riding a bike that's too small, for instance, is like walking in a half-squat: very fatiguing. Bikes aren't like cars, 'one size and type fits all', they're like shoes. And like shoes, you need different bikes for different activities. You don't go mountaineering in a pair of flip flops, or running in a pair of cowboy boots.

Cycling is fun. But to enjoy it fully you need the right bike and the know-how to set it up to suit you and the type of cycling you're doing.

MODERN BIKES

The bicycle has remained unchanged in its basic design for around 100 years. The frame is still a double-triangle design, and the bike is still chain driven to the rear wheel. What we have seen is ever more specialization. There are bikes for racing, touring, shopping, jumping around on – whatever you fancy. There are even some which depart radically from the basic design; we'll look at those on page 26.

Road bikes

Road bikes are the greyhounds of the cycling world, as they are capable of being ridden at high speeds on smooth surfaces and weigh in at just 18–25lb (8.5–11.3kg). Tyres are pencil thin and pumped up to over 100psi to provide minimal friction on the road, and the dropped handlebars – sometimes supplemented with the arms-out-in-front tri bars – allow a wind-cheating position to be adopted. A good rider will average above 20mph on a road bike, even over distances of 100–200 miles.

The road bike is built with a short wheelbase and steep frame angles, giving it quick handling, so that it turns at the flick of the handlebar, and providing excellent transfer of power whether the rider is seated or standing.

Road bikes were often known as ten speeds in the '70s and early '80s, but now typically have 14 or 16 gears, with two chainrings and seven or eight cogs at the rear. Nine rear cogs made an appearance in 1996, while three chainrings are occasionally used for Alpine-

style riding. Gears are indexed, and on better bikes are operated from behind the brake levers.

Road bikes don't usually feature mudguards (cheaper ones, used as training bikes during the winter, often have them) or racks. Variations include the time-trial bike and the cyclo-cross bike. The design of the time trial bike – on which one man races against the clock – is much more aerodynamic, putting the rider in a less comfortable (but more streamlined) position, and has a smaller spread of gears. The cyclo-cross bike is a more rugged road bike with knobbled tyres.

Road bikes are designed to be ridden fast on smooth roads. The handlebars allow you to adopt an aerodynamic tuck, and the high-pressure tyres are slick to provide minimal friction.

Low gears, good brakes and an easy rid-ing position have made mountain bikes the recreational bike for the '80s and '90s. The fat knobbly tyres are comfortable, and offer lots of traction off-road but too much fric-tion on road.

Mountain bikes

The all-terrain vehicle of the bike world, the mountain bike has overtaken the road bike as *the* bike that everyone buys. Over 80% of bikes sold are mountain bikes (MTBs) – yet they were only invented in the mid '70s, and when they were introduced to the bike trade in 1981 their American inventors were told they'd never catch on. The MTB is unmistakable: chunky tyres, 26-inch wheels, strong frame, flat or slightly upswept handlebars, 21 or 24 gears to get you up and down any hill, and brakes with immense stopping power.

The original bikes were modified 40-year-old fat-tyre cruisers, weighing in at 45lb (20.4kg). Today's are made from steel alloy or aluminium and often weigh under 25lb (11.3kg). Technology is seeping across to them from the motorcycle world, and devices such as suspension and disc brakes are starting to gain popularity.

A word on pseudo-MTBs: the popularity of mountain bikes means that there are many that look the part that cost under £200. There's nothing wrong with these bikes as long as you realize their limi-tations. They're okay for cruising around the street, but are ultimately too heavy, too over-geared and occasionally just too badly made for serious off-road riding.

Touring bikes

The touring bike is essentially a road bike that's more comfortable, more sedate, and better at carrying luggage. Dropped handlebars still fea-ture as they offer a variety of hand positions, which is useful for long days in the saddle, but tyres are fatter and more rugged.

All tourers have a wide range of gears (three chainrings), so that you can get the greater load of bike-plus-luggage up hills more easily. Brakes are powerful cantilevers, like a mountain bike's.

Probably the most versatile bike, the tourer is designed to be ridden long distances in comfort, and to carry luggage. Equally at home crossing town as crossing Africa.

Wheelbase is longer than a road bike and frame angles are shallower. This gives a bike that irons out bumps in the road, and handles predictably even when laden with panniers. Touring bikes come with a minimum of mudguards and a rack.

Sales of touring bikes are relatively low, yet for many cyclists the tourer is the perfect compromise. You can ride it all day, on roads or bridle-ways, and it's the best standard bike for load-carrying – whether that's camping gear or a week's shopping.

MODERN BIKES CONT.

Hybrid bikes

The hybrid is a cross between a mountain bike and a utility bike. It has the looks of a mountain bike, but with skinnier, larger (27-inch) wheels. Its origin lies in the fact that most mountain bike owners rarely ride off-road. Tractor-style tyres and ruggedness are therefore not required.

The upright riding position of the hybrid makes it a good urban bike, and if it doesn't come equipped with all the commuting essentials like mudguards, rack, and lights, it can easily be fitted with them. Sporty hybrids come with the MTB's triple chainrings and derailleurs; practical hybrids with the utility bike's internal hub gears.

The hybrid is an urbanised mountain bike. It's like the tourer in that it can go off-road, but is designed for the road.

Utility bikes

The most popular bike world-wide, the utility bike is a cheap, simple form of transport for urban areas. You see it everywhere from China and Africa to the Netherlands. It has a sit-up-and-beg riding style and features mudguards, a chainguard and usually a three-speed hub gear. Step-through frames are common.

This bike has existed for decades; many old ones, in fact, are still in service to this day. These old-style bikes are tremendously heavy, often black, and have rod-operated stirrup style brakes

The best equipped modern utility bikes tend to be of Dutch origin. The classiest and most durable are the old-style roadsters, which are still being made today. Avoid the small-wheeled shopper bikes from the '70s.

The American utility bike of the 1950s has been resurrected, in the wake of the mountain bike which it inspired, as today's cruiser.

BMX

Before the mountain bike, there was the BMX. The BMX is a little bike with 20-inch wheels, knobbly tyres, a single gear and a rugged light-weight frame.

BMX stands for Bicycle Motocross, the primary use of these bikes: racing around a short dirt track full of bumps and bends. BMXs are also used for 'freestyle' activities – balancing on one wheel, leaping into the air etc. This kind of BMXing has more in common with skateboarding than cycling.

From an adult's point of view, BMXs are fine for their dedicated uses (tricks or dirt races) but useless as transportation. For children, a BMX is a good precursor to a mountain bike, and often a better and lighter machine than the standard child's bike.

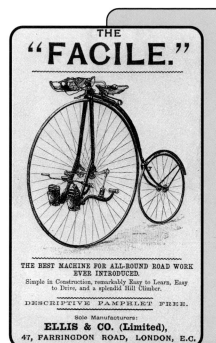

THE
"FACILE."

THE BEST MACHINE FOR ALL-ROUND ROAD WORK EVER INTRODUCED.

Simple in Construction, remarkably Easy to Learn, Easy to Drive, and a splendid Hill Climber.

DESCRIPTIVE PAMPHLET FREE.

Sole Manufacturers:
ELLIS & CO. (Limited),
47, FARRINGDON ROAD, LONDON, E.C.

Early bikes

The very first rideable bicycle was invented by a German, Baron Karl von Drais, in 1817. The bike had two wheels attached to a padded wooden beam where the rider sat, a handle-bar, but no pedals; the rider pushed himself along with his feet.

It was over 20 years later before ped-als, or rather treadles, were included in the design of the bicycle. Scottish blacksmith Kirkpatrick Macmillan produced a bicycle with treadles attached to the rear wheel in 1839. The bike worked well – Macmillan did one journey of 140 miles on it, but it never caught on.

It was left for a French coach builder, Pierre Michaux, to set the wheels turning again in 1861 when he fitted pedals and cranks to the front wheel. Michaux's 'velocipede' was a big hit, and was refined further during the remainder of the decade. Developments included metal spoked wheels, solid rubber tyre and an increase in the size of the front wheel.

To go faster and further for each turn of the pedals, the wheel had to get bigger. Which accounted for the Ordinary bicycle, or Penny Farthing, popular in Britain in the 1870s. An Ordinary bicycle was ridden around the world from 1884 to 1887 by American Thomas Stevens, yet the design had failings: the size of the gear was the size of the front wheel, which was re-stricted by the length of the rider's inside leg; and the riding position was dangerous.

In 1885, John Kemp Starley launched the Rover Safety bicycle, which was chain driven to the rear wheel. By having a large chainring and a small sprocket the wheel could be made smaller without forcing the rider to twiddle along in a tiny gear. And the rider could adopt a safer riding position – one that's still used to this day.

Folding bikes

Folding bikes are designed for mixed-mode transport, travelling as luggage in trains, planes or taxis. They trade some riding convenience for portability of course, but are great for short trips, and enable you to ride where you would other-wise have to walk.

Cheap folders are a nightmare: heavy, awk-ward to fold, and absolutely horrible to ride. More expensive folders, such as the Brompton, are excellent. The Brompton rides well, and folds through an ingenious process of bicycle origami to a package measuring just 57 x 56 x 26cm (approx 22½ x 22 x10in).

BICYCLE ANATOMY

Compared to an internal combustion engine, a bicycle is a simple machine. The great benefit of this is that it doesn't take much technical knowledge to choose the best bike for you. But you must know your way around the basics.

The bike illustrated is a hybrid; the details are common to most others. If you come across any terms that aren't explained in detail here, refer to the glossary (page 188) and also to the relevant maintenance section.

A. Top tube
B. Down tube
C. Head tube
D. Seat tube
E. Chain stays
F. Seat stays
G. Drop outs
H. Saddle
I. Brake lever
J. Brake cable
K. Cranks
L. Spider
M. Hub
N. Spoke
O. Spoke nipple
P. Chain

1. Frame. The double-triangle design is simple and structurally stiff; bikes with open frames ('women's bikes') tend to be flexible, which means that some pedalling energy is absorbed by the frame.

Most frames are made from metal alloys, usually steel but sometimes aluminium or titanium. They are most commonly lugged-and-brazed or TIG-welded. In the former, the tubes are brazed (a process like soldering, but hotter) into pre-cut metal lugs; in the latter, the tubes are welded together. Other methods include fillet brazing, without lugs, and bonding (gluing).

Frame angles are crucial to a bike's handling; for more on this see page 160.

2. Forks. The bike's forks are crucial to its handling. Other things being equal, a shallow head tube angle that makes the forks less vertical gives more stable steering. A steeper angle makes the steering response more immediate, but requires rider concentration. To see the effect of a really shallow head tube angle, watch how a motorcycle chopper turns.

3. Braze-ons. The non-structural extra bits on the frame, including cable guides, and eyelets for attaching racks, mudguards and bottle cages.

4. Handlebars. Dropped bars are used on road bikes and tourers, flat bars on MTBs and hybrids. Flat bars are limited in offering only one hand position, and so many MTBs have 'bar ends' added. Brake and gear levers are in easy reach.

5. Derailleur. Used to shift the chain from one chainring or sprocket to another, they are so called because they 'de-rail' the chain. Derailleurs are cable-operated and work by a simple parallelogram principle. The rear derailleur has a tensioning arm to take up the slack in the chain when the smaller sprockets and/or chainrings are being used.

6. Headset. The bearings at each end of the head tube that allow the fork to turn in the head tube, and so steer the bike.

7. Seat post. Height can and should be adjusted to suit the size of the rider. The saddle's angle and fore and aft position are also adjustable.

8. Bottom bracket. The bottom bracket shell houses the axle on which the cranks turn.

9. Chainrings. One on roadsters, BMXs and some hybrids, two on road bikes, and three on mountain bikes, most hybrids, and tourers.

The bigger the chainring and the smaller the sprocket, the more times the wheel will turn with every revolution of the cranks – which is better for powering along at speed. Conversely, the smaller the chainring and the larger the sprocket, the easier it is to ride uphill.

10. Cassette. A set of seven or eight sprockets (or cogs) of different sizes that fit on the rear hub, called a freehub. You can fit different sprockets or chainrings to change the gearing.

11. Stem. The stem clamps the handlebars and attaches to the end of the fork, which passes up through the head tube. The height and angle of the stem determine where the handlebars will go, and hence how stretched out and/or how upright the cyclist will ride. Conventional stems can be raised up or down to suit; A-headset-style stems found on many MTBs and hybrids cannot.

12. Gear cable. A woven steel cable that operates a derailleur as the lever variously pulls it and eases off. Cable-housing keeps the cable in tension around bends.

13. Gear lever. Sometimes called a shifter. Modern levers are 'indexed', which allows simple click up, click down gear changing.

14. Rim. Once a steel hoop, now an alloy one on all good bikes. The rim additionally provides the braking surface for brake blocks.

15. Tyre. Different widths, treads and tyre pressures are used on different bikes. A mountain bike may use a knobbled tyre as wide as 60mm (approx 2½in), while road bike tyres are smooth, higher pressure, and as narrow as 18mm (approx ¾in).

16. Inner tube. The air-filled inner of the tyre. Two valve types predominate: Schraeder (car valve type) and, for high pressure tyres, Presta.

17. Brakes. Most brakes work on the wheel rim and consist of a lever, one or more cables, two blocks, a pivot arrangement, and springs to keep the blocks off the rim after they've been applied. Cantilever brakes (shown) are simple and effective, and are found on hybrids, MTBs and tourers. Road bikes use calliper brakes. For other types of brakes, see page 158.

18. Bearings. To minimize friction the headset, hubs, pedals and bottom bracket have greased steel ball bearings, often held together in a cage, rolling in between the two bearing surfaces.

19. Pedal. On better road bikes and MTBs, clipless pedals hold the cycling shoe secure, rather like the clip-in bindings on a ski. Many tourers use a flat pedal with a toe-clip. Roadsters, BMXs and hybrids have flat pedals for use with ordinary shoes.

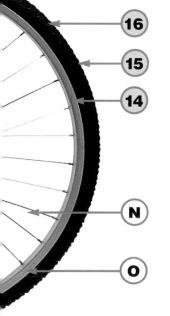

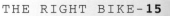

WHICH BIKE?

Do you buy this Rockgobbler MTB or that Loghopper? With so many bikes available it can be bewildering making the initial choice. The good news is that the question 'which specific bike should I buy?' can wait: several bikes at the same price might be equally good. The question you must ask is what you want to use the bike *for*.

Why choose a road bike?

Get a road bike if you're going to do any kind of road racing, or if you want to get fit. Even professional mountain bikers use road bikes for fitness work.

Road bikes are also good for long distance commuting – 10 miles (16km) or more each way – simply because they're quicker. For urban riding, you'll need to fit heavier, wider tyres to prevent punctures.

Road bikes are good for fast leisure cycling, and even light touring, but in this case look for a road bike with a triple chainring (Giant do several) and eyes for a rack and mudguards.

For a basic road bike, you'll need to spend £300 plus. At this point you should expect the top, down, seat and head tubes to be good steel – either chromoly or Reynolds 531. Gears are likely to be a Shimano indexed model with down tube shifters.

Forget stationary exercise bikes: if you want to get fit, get a road bike.

Why choose a mountain bike?

The mountain bike is the four-wheel drive of the bike world: great off-road, but neither comfortable nor quick on road. Get a mountain bike for any kind of off-road racing, or if you plan to do a lot of rough-stuff riding.

If fitted with slick tyres and mudguards, an MTB makes a good urban bike, but more expensive ones are thief magnets. MTBs can be used for touring, but unless you're going to be riding off-road most of the time a touring bike is much more comfortable.

Again, expect to pay £300 and upwards. At the time of writing the best value mountain bike on the market is the Saracen Rufftrax. On a basic MTB, you can expect chromoly tubing, Shimano Alivio or Acera gears and alloy wheels. A double chainring on an MTB usually signifies a real donkey.

Why choose a tourer?

Get a tourer if you plan to go on cycling holidays; it will carry your luggage easily, and you comfortably. It's also a good choice if you'll mainly be using your bike for leisure cycling or as daily transport.

For short distance urban cycling, you might be better off with a utility bike or hybrid, but if you're riding far a tourer is a better choice.

Touring bikes don't sell to casual purchasers, and perhaps because of this prices start higher. Expect to pay around £500–£600 for a bike with Reynolds 531ST tubing, and a mix of Shimano components.

Why choose a hybrid?

If you're not going to be racing (on road or off) or riding 50 miles or more in a day, the hybrid is a good choice – better than a mountain bike for

For racing and for the roughest kinds of off-road riding, a proper mountain bike is the only option. With a few modifications it'll make a good town bike too.

QUICK FACT

You don't have to have a mountain bike to go off-road. Tourers and hybrids can handle bridleways, while the cyclo-cross bike is an adapted road bike.

the majority of cyclists. In Britain, the lack of decent utility bikes makes the hybrid a good candidate for a city run-around too.

Like mountain bikes, you really need to spend around £300 to get a decent hybrid. Frame, gears etc won't be quite as good as a same-price MTB as hybrids come with extras like a rack, mudguards and sometimes lights.

Why choose a utility bike?

Get a utility bike if you only want to go a short distance from A to B over fairly flat terrain, in all weathers. The upright position is perfect for riding in traffic. If you live in a hilly area, or want to ride off-road too, you'll appreciate the extra gears of a hybrid.

Second-hand, you might be able to pick up an old rod-brake equipped roadster cheaply. Pashley (in Stratford-on-Avon, England) still make new ones. Other good utility bikes are hard to find – the Dutch are the only Europeans to make them in any numbers – so you might be better off with a hybrid.

BUYING A NEW BIKE

There's only one golden rule for buying a new bike: go to a good bike shop. You will pay slightly more compared to a discount warehouse, or a shop that sells bikes and toys. It will be worth every penny.

A good shop will give you a guarantee, and will give you advice and service after you've bought the bike. If you want to buy your bike with accessories fitted, or parts changed, then a good shop will do this at point of sale. No problem.

Above: Getting a bike by mail order is a bad move for beginners, though cyclists who know exactly what they're after can save money this way.

Finding a good shop

Ask other local cyclists; the reputation of a good shop will precede it. Your local library may hold details of the nearest cycling club. Alternatively, visit your local bike shops. Assess whether the staff are pleasant, knowledgeable and enthusiastic. Try asking for something obscure like a six-speed screw-on SunTour block, and see what they say.

Look for signs of commitment to the cycling world: advertisements for second-hand bikes; fliers for forthcoming club runs or races; people in cycling gear (with shaved legs) chatting with the staff. If the staff care about cycling, they'll care about selling you the right bike.

When you've found your shop, explain what sort of bike you're looking for, and why you want it. (Cycling magazines can help you make a more informed purchase here.) If they haven't got the exact model you want, ask. They might be able to order it for you, or they might have an equally suitable model in stock.

Final checks

It's worth making some of the checks listed on page 20 for second-hand bikes. A new bike is unlikely to have suffered crash damage, but Friday night specials with, say, badly aligned frames are more common than you'd think.

By going to a good shop you minimize the chances of brakes or gears being set up badly or being defective, or the bottom bracket or headset being packed without grease but problems can occur, and it's best to spot them early. Ideally before you pay.

Many good shops will allow you to take a test ride. Do it. But you must expect to leave adequate security with them.

A good bike shop won't just sell you any bike. It's in their interest to sell you the right bike, so that you keep cycling and become a regular customer.

What about mail order?

Mail order firms are a hit and miss affair. Some are great, some awful. The advantage of using them is that you get the bike cheap. The disadvantage is that you often get the bike disassembled, and you can't walk into a shop and kick up a fuss if anything goes wrong. Sorting out teething problems can take a long time – you are on your own.

In general, if you're an experienced cyclist you can save a lot of money by buying mail order, though you may have to sort out some minor problems when the new bike arrives. If you're a beginner, mail order can be a nightmare. Go to a shop.

If you do buy a bike mail order, try to pay by instalments. They are more likely to help you if you owe them money.

TIPS

> Be realistic about the kind of equipment to expect on a new bike. No manufacturer can offer something for nothing. If there are two mountain bikes at the same price, one with suspension forks and one without, chances are the one without is the better bike. Why? Because decent suspension forks cost a lot. The suspension forks on a £400 bike must be cheap and are probably very nasty. Yet they will also be more expensive for the manufacturer to fit than rigid forks, so corners will have to be cut elsewhere on the bike. You lose both ways.

> Never, ever buy a new sub-£100 bike. It will be awful. You have been warned.

BUYING A SECOND-HAND BIKE

You can nearly always get a better bike for less money if you buy second-hand. But first you have to track down a suitable bike in your size, and then you need to be sure it's not stolen or damaged.

Most local newspapers carry advertisements for bikes. The bulk of them are cheap ones, so you may have to wait for something good to come up. Some bike shops have a board advertising second-hand bikes; these will be closer to what you're after. Most cycling magazines carry adverts too; the disadvantage is that you may have to travel to see the bike.

Checking out the bike

When you go to inspect the bike, take a friend for support, technical knowledge (if yours is lacking), and to wait with the seller while you go for a test ride. Remember to take along some cash for a deposit. If you pay solely by cheque, the seller may want to hold on to the bike until your cheque has cleared.

Before you hand over any money, ask to see the frame number. It's usually on the bottom bracket shell under the cable guides, or on the rear drop out. If it's been filed off the bike is probably stolen. Alert the police. If it's there, get the seller to write out a receipt for you with the frame number and their name and address on it.

Find out what the purchase price was so you know what you're saving. You should expect to save 30% or more. But be suspicious if a quality bike seems *too* cheap.

If you're buying a derailleur geared bike that's several years old, be aware that the standard number of sprockets has increased. If you want to use modern components on a five-speed frame you'll need the rear drop outs widened by a frame builder (cost: around £20).

The checks listed below aren't exhaustive, but should reveal common problems. Insist on a test ride, and while you're on it, change gears, use the brakes and so forth.

What to look for

1. Crash damage
Rippled paint on the top and down tubes where they meet the head tube suggests crash damage. Do not buy the bike.

2. Frame alignment
Try riding the bike hands off, if you are able to, on your test ride. If the bike consistently veers to one side the frame is out of line. Do not buy.

3. Are wheels true?
Lift front and then back wheels off the ground and spin them. Any side to side movement? The wheels will need truing, either by you (see page 122) or a shop. Bulges or cracks in the rim will require a wheel rebuild.

4. Bent forks

Check that the forks aren't bent inwards towards the down tube; check the top of the forks carefully. Then look at them head on to see if the wheel sits equidistant between them.

5. Rear wheel alignment

Check the seat stays aren't bent and that the wheel sits equidistant between them. While you're there, be sure to check that the derailleur hanger is vertical.

6. Worn gear set

Hooked teeth on the chainrings or sprockets are a sign of wear. Try to pull the chain off the chainring from the front; if it lifts as high as the top of the teeth it's worn. Replacing cassette, chain and chainrings will cost £50 minimum.

7. Worn headset

Hold the bars, apply the front brake and rock the bike. If it feels loose, the headset is either too loose or worn. Lift the bars to get the wheel in the air, and turn left and right. Any sticking? The headset is too tight, or worn.

8. Bent pedal spindle

The pedal spindles should be parallel to the floor and at right angles to the down tube. If not, you need new pedals or – less likely – new cranks.

9. General wear

Frayed cable ends, a ripped saddle, and torn bar tape are signs that the bike may not have been looked after. Worn tyres or brake blocks will need replacing.

SIZING YOUR BIKE

You must ride a bike that you're comfortable on. At the very least, try the bike for size in the shop. Better still, do some homework with a tape measure and a calculator beforehand.

Rough and ready method

Straddle the bike. Your crotch should clear the top tube by 1–2in (2½–5cm approx) for road bike, about 1in (2½cm approx) for a tourer, and 3in (7½cm approx) or more for a mountain bike or hybrid.

The saddle is too low if you can touch the floor with both feet. Raise it so that, with your heel on the pedal, your leg is fully extended. Remember to pedal with the ball of your foot.

Assume your normal riding position. If you feel too cramped, you need a longer stem; if too stretched, a shorter stem, perhaps with a higher rise.

Scientific method

To get a more precise fit, apply the system developed by Bernard Hinault and Claude Genzling in their book *Road Racing Technique and Training*. Their guide is an extremely useful starting point, but you should listen to your body too, and do what's comfortable.

Get a friend to measure your inside leg. Wearing cycling shorts, stand with your back to a wall with your bare feet about 4 inches (10cm approx) apart. Your friend should use a flat marker (an LP record or a book), and hold it against the wall so it just contacts your crotch. Step away from the wall. Measure the distance to the floor. Repeat three times and take the average. This is your inside leg.

Finding your frame size (road bikes)

Multiply your inside leg by 0.65. This should be your approximate frame size. Frame size is found by measuring along the seat tube from the centre of the bottom bracket to the centre of the top tube.

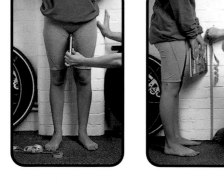

Get a friend to help measure your inside leg (see Scientific method). This measurement shows what size road frame you need; an MTB frame needs to be about 2 inches smaller.

Positioning your saddle

To find the ideal distance between the centre of the bottom bracket and the top of your saddle, multiply your inside leg by 0.885. Next, using a plumbline, set the nose of the saddle back behind the centre of the bottom bracket by the distance shown in the table.

Positioning your handlebars

The reach from the nose of your saddle to the handlebars where the stem clamps them should be in the range shown in the

How to size your road bike

Inside leg length	Frame size (inches in brackets)	Saddle setback	Saddle height	Handlebar reach	Handlebar height	Crank length (mm)
72–75	47–49 (18–19)	3–5	64–66	42–50	4–5	160
75–78	49–51 (19–20)	4–6	66–69	46–55	5–6	162.5
79–82	51–53 (20–21)	5–7	70–73	49–57	6–7	165
83–86	54–56 (21–22)	6–8	73–76	52–59	7–8	170–172.5
87–90	57–59 (22–23)	7–9	77–80	54–60	8–9	175–177.5
91–94	59–61 (23–24)	8–10	81–83	57–63	9–10	180

All figures in cm, except crank length (mm). Frame size is also given in inches in brackets.

QUICK FACT

Like suits, bikes can be custom made to fit you. Expect to pay from £400 for the frame, or £700 plus for a whole bike.

table on the opposite page. If you have a short upper body and long legs, start near the lower end of the range. If you have a relatively long upper body you'll need a greater reach; start near the upper end.

The height of your handlebars (see table) is the vertical distance between the top of the bars and the top of your saddle, with the saddle being set higher. The width of your handlebars should be about the width of your shoulders.

The right crank length

To pedal comfortably and efficiently, crank length should be about one fifth of your inside leg (see table).

When straddling the bike you should be able to put your feet flat on the floor and still clear the top tube, otherwise you're asking for a nasty accident.

Sizing other bikes

For a mountain bike, knock off a couple of inches (or 5cm) to get the frame size. Mountain bikes need more top tube clearance, and more seatpost exposed. Other measurements are okay as a starting point, but you may need to experiment until you get comfortable. In particular, if you're not a racer, you may find the handlebars too low.

For touring bikes, hybrids and especially utility bikes, you will want the handlebars higher – perhaps above the level of the saddle – and the reach shorter.

FINE TUNING

If you're lucky, setting up your bike according to the guidelines on the previous pages will be all you need to do. If you're not – particularly if you're not built on average lines – you'll need to do some fine tuning.

Reach for your bars

Wide handlebars give more control – good for MTB downhilling and loaded touring – but are awkward in traffic. Generally, as stated previously, handlebars should be about as wide as your shoulders.

Dropped bars need to be purchased in the appropriate size. Flat bars don't. Most come sized for the average gorilla, but it's simple to hacksaw an inch or two off each end.

If you suffer from wrist ache with flat bars, try fitting bar ends to give you an alternate hand position. If it fails, and likewise if you get wrist ache with dropped bars, you're probably putting too much weight on your hands. Try a shorter, more upright stem. This can also be an antidote to persistent lower back pain.

If you're too cramped, fit a longer stem. But if you need a stem longer than about 5 inches (12cm approx) the bike's handling may suffer; the so-called 'tiller effect'. Get a bike with a longer top tube – basically this means a bigger bike. Likewise, if even the shortest stem leaves you feeling too stretched, you need a shorter top tube (i.e. a smaller bike).

If you have a long torso for your height, you may need to fit a longer stem for comfort. If you want to sit more upright, try a shorter and/or more upright stem.

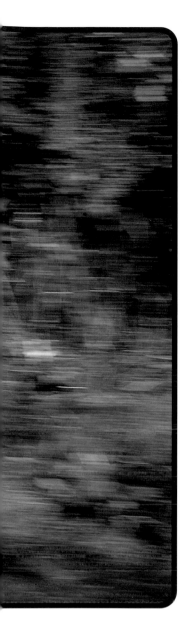

Above: Cycling is not an uncomfortable sport. If something aches, something's wrong. This cyclist looks a bit too stretched out.

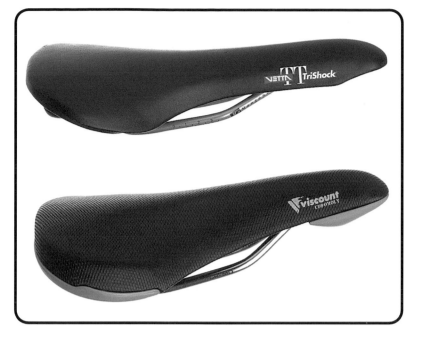

Some people like narrow, cutaway saddles, others wider ones, others sprung saddles. Experiment with your friends' bikes and fit whatever is comfortable.

Sitting comfortably

Novice cyclists often get a sore backside. If this doesn't ease, and you're already wearing cycling shorts, sort out your saddle.

The angle of the saddle should initially be set to horizontal. If you tip the nose up it may cause numbness and/or pain in the genital area; if you tip it down more than a little, you may find you slip forward and place too much weight on your wrists.

What's comfortable in a saddle is a personal thing. If you want a broad sprung saddle on your mountain bike, fit one! If you get on better with a narrow racy saddle, use one. Don't assume that the saddle supplied with your bike is the best one for the job. It's a case of trial and error.

If the whole bike still feels too 'harsh', try fitting wider tyres. The larger air pocket will have a greater cushioning effect

Bikes for women

Bikes are generally built by men for men. Women are poorly catered for. Unless you're planning to ride in a skirt, there's no reason why you shouldn't ride a bike with a top tube, and a good structural reason why you should: the bike is stiffer. This helps not only with the transfer of pedalling energy, but makes the bike less wobbly if you're carrying a load on the back.

Women have longer legs in relation to their bodies than men, which means that a bike sized on leg length will be the right height (seat tube) but too long (top tube). The simplest way around this is to use a smaller frame with the right reach, and then use a longer seat post and set the stem a bit higher.

A woman's pelvis is broader than a man's, so you'll need a dedicated woman's saddle. Terry saddles are among the best – Selle Italia and Brooks do some good ones too.

Bikes for the short and the tall

The problem that shorter riders have is that road bikes, tourers, utility bikes and hybrids all come with big (700C) wheels. You can't get wheels this big into a frame under about 19 inches (48cm). Tough break if your inside leg is under 29 inches (74cm).

Mountain bikes, with their smaller wheels, aren't a problem. They come in sizes down to about 14 inches. You may need to fit smaller cranks if the manufacturers have overlooked them, and adjust the brake levers to put them nearer the bars where you can reach them. Also, since you'll be using shorter cranks, you'll have less leverage when pedalling so you'll need slightly smaller gears across the board. Fit smaller chainrings.

For a small road bike or tourer, the cheapest option is probably to buy a mountain bike frame, then kit it out with slick tyres and dropped handlebars. A few manufacturers (Cannondale, Orbit, Terry Precision) offer off-the-peg bikes with 26-inch wheels. Most custom framebuilders could do you a suitable bike too.

For tall riders, the problem is that as the frame gets larger it gets more flexible. You need a bike made from sterner stuff. Look for oversize (larger diameter) tubing – either aluminium or steel. If you are really huge, get advice from a frame-builder.

THE WEIRD AND THE WONDERFUL

So far we've only looked at the most common kinds of bikes. Yet there's a huge range of pedal-driven vehicles available, serving all needs and obsessions. Here's a brief run down.

Recumbent trikes are expensive, due to the small numbers being made. But they're great fun to ride, and are fully road-legal.

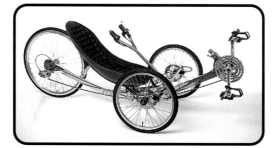

Recumbents

Often touted as the bike of the future, recumbents may yet become just that. The rider sits in a supported seat in a reclined position, with the pedals out in front. It's extremely comfortable, being much kinder on backs, necks and wrists than the traditional cycling position.

Recumbents can be very aerodynamic. The best racing recumbents are as aero as a time trial machine, and if equipped with fairings (body coverings) can outstrip any conventional bike. The furthest anyone has travelled on an upright bike in one hour is around 56km (35 miles approx). The furthest anyone has travelled on a recumbent in one hour is around 76km (47 miles approx). Both records change hands regularly, but the record for a conventional bicycle is always held by a professional cyclist; whereas amateurs are able to compete for the recumbent record.

There's a huge diversity in recumbent design: short-wheelbase racing machines; long-wheelbase tourers; tricycles that can be equipped with body shells for all-weather riding; even load-luggers like the Pickup (see below).

Recumbents have got everything in their favour except price. Small scale production means high prices. Expect to pay at least £800 for an entry-level two-wheeler, the Ross SWB or the Linear LWB, or about £2,000 for a trike.

Track bikes

A track bike is a road bike stripped down to its bare essentials: a single gear, no brakes and also no freewheel mechanism. Its primary use is in track races, which take place on a 250m (270yd) banked track.

If fitted with a front brake, it's legal to ride a track bike on the open road. But it takes some getting used to. You cannot freewheel. I'll repeat that: you cannot freewheel. You must pedal through every corner, and continue pedalling downhill, and even when you're slowing down. Ride a track bike on the road and you will learn a lot about pedalling.

Track bikes are popular with some cycle-couriers, who say that they're easier to maintain (definitely true – fewer moving parts), are less fatiguing on flat city roads (maybe), and that they give you better bike control (eventually). Such couriers can stop by flicking the back wheel in the air, locking the cranks, and then grounding the static back wheel. Do not try this.

Carrier cycles

The argument that private cars are necessary for carrying loads around is blown to bits by the current breed of transporter bikes. Even the old butchers' bikes with a small front wheel and huge basket could carry moderate loads (such bikes are still made by Pashley, incidentally).

Danish bikes like the two-wheeled Long John and the High Box Transporter trike will carry beer barrels, children, sacks of cement, an ice-cream seller's box – you name it. A couple of British quadricycles can do better still. The Brox and Pickup can each carry around 200kg, or 440lb.

Tandems

Tandems offer twice the power of a solo bike with the same wind resistance. On the flat or going downhill a tandem will overtake anything, though it is a bit slower going up.

A tandem is a great machine for two riders of differing ability, since no one is going to be left behind. It's also a good investment for cycling families, since simple adaptations allow even a four-year-old to sit in the rear seat and pedal.

Getting used to a tandem doesn't take too long, and offers a unique cycling experience. Most owners swear by them, not at them. Three, four and even five-seater tandems are available. A budget two-seater (by far the most common type) will cost about £650; quality ones can cost two or three times that price.

Trikes

Trikes are heavier, slower and more expensive than solo bikes. Yet they do have advantages: you can carry a lot more on a full-sized trike, and you can also cycle at 0.5mph – or even remain stationary – without falling off.

Trikes tend to be more popular among the old and/or infirm, but some individualistic cyclists do race and tour on them. Racing is just plain scary. Trikes cannot be leant over on corners like bikes; instead you have to lean out over the road, like a yachtsman with something hard to fall on. For more information contact the Tricycle Association 0113 260 5290.

Unicycles

Unicycles are great for spangly-trousered street-jugglers, but of limited practical use. New ones cost around £100.

The word tandem comes from the Latin for 'at length'. Side-by-sides do exist, but mostly as curiosities rather than as serious bikes. Off-road tandems are difficult to ride on rough terrain.

HIT THE ROAD

Riding a bike is something you never forget how to do. But riding a bike on the road in traffic is something that many cyclists never learn. The fact that there is no test to pass before you can venture out onto the roads makes it more important to learn traffic skills, not less. You are a vulnerable road user, and your safety is primarily in your own hands.

Your bike

Ride a bike that fits you so you can control it properly. And maintain it so that the brakes won't fail at a junction. For an urban bike, an upright riding position is best. You are less aerodynamic, but with your head high your field of vision is better; you can even see over cars.

If you ride in all weathers, fit mudguards. They may not be stylish, but nor is a skunk stripe of dirty water up your back. Hub gears are great in town as you can change down while you're waiting at traffic lights. A rack and panniers (alternatively a courier bag) are essential for luggage. Never dangle a bag from your handlebars; if it goes into the front wheel you will catapult yourself into the road.

Cycle paths are becoming more common. Some are good, some bad. You are not obliged to use a bad path, or even a good one; you can still use the road.

A bell or horn is useful for alerting jaywalking pedestrians, though if you want to alert motorists you'll need a pressurised air-horn or a referee's whistle (any audible warning device is legal). Or you can shout. A mirror can be helpful for traffic riding, but is not a substitute for taking a good look behind.

Basic skills

You must be able to stop and start easily, steer accurately, ride with one hand on the bars, and be able to look around you to check for traffic. These skills are easy to learn.

A harder skill to learn is traffic awareness. If you already drive a car, then you have a head start. If not, then either take the National Cycling Proficiency Test (ask at schools or libraries) or go out on the road with an experienced cyclist and ride behind them. If you live in London, contact The London School of Cycling for information (0171 730 3450).

Many car drivers don't know the correct way to behave around cyclists as they are very unlikely to have been tested on the cycling section in the Highway Code. The problem is compounded where the cyclist is unsure too. Learn the rules, and the skills to use them, and apply them.

Don't be timid and cling to the side of the road. Ride at least two or three feet out or drivers will come alongside you and force you into the gutter. Make your presence felt. This is the key to successful cycling in traffic.

In any manoeuvre, eyeball the relevant driver, signal boldly, and when the coast is clear go where you want to go without dithering. If you are definite and obvious in what you are doing, other road users will treat you with respect.

With the right gear, you can commute in comfort in most weather, and you'll arrive more invigorated than if you'd driven.

Act like traffic, be treated like traffic – because you *are* traffic, and you have as much right to be on the road as anyone.

Route finding

Using minor roads on a bicycle rarely costs you any speed, and is both more pleasant and safer. Plan your daily journeys to avoid big roads where possible. An A to Z is useful for any big town or city, but rights of way are not shown, and neither are some lanes. Ordnance Survey maps (1: 50,000 Landranger and 1: 25,000 Pathfinder) are worth getting for you local area.

The law

Like any other road user, you must obey traffic signals – this means round signs with a red border, traffic lights, Give Way signs, road markings etc. Ignore these and you can be prosecuted.

Although The Highway Code details some traffic laws, it is not in itself law. But if you don't obey the Code and you cause an accident, then the fact that you ignored it may (and probably will) be held against you. Get a copy from any bookshop and read it.

Before you start to turn right, check behind to see if the way's clear. You may be able to start your turn if the traffic is a long way off, or slow moving. But don't take chances.

RIDING SKILLS

Safe cycling doesn't only come from experience. Good practice can be applied as soon as you venture out onto the road.

Right turns

Look behind *early*. If the road is empty, move out into the centre of the road, just left of the white line. Where possible try to time your move so there's no traffic coming towards you either, and then you won't have to wait in the middle of the road.

If there's a lot of traffic, eyeball the driver behind you, signal clearly, and start to move out. Keep your eye on that driver. If he tries to come around you, let him. Either he's seen you and has decided to come past anyway, or (less likely) he hasn't seen you at all. Keep signalling, and keep eyeballing drivers. Someone will let you out.

When you make your turn into the side road, go into the left-hand lane. Do not cut the corner. An oncoming car could hit you, and you would be in the wrong.

At a T-junction, place yourself in the middle of the road, left of the centre line. Wait until a gap in both lanes of traffic appears, then cross.

Left turns

Don't hug the kerb on the approach to a left turn. Signal early and clearly. Any following traffic which is also turning left is less likely to squeeze you into the gutter.

If you're going straight ahead, beware cars cutting across in front of you to turn left. If they misjudge your speed you will crash into the side of the car. They are more likely to cut you up the further left you are.

Beware cars coming out of side roads on your left. Again, the further to the left you are, the less likely they are to see you, especially if there are parked cars, walls or trees around. When you get closer, eyeball the driver to ensure that he has seen you.

Overtaking

When you're overtaking parked cars or slower vehicles, check behind early, signal, and move out at a gradual angle. If you leave it to the last minute, you risk swerving into the path of a car that's overtaking you at the same time. Don't weave in and out when overtaking a line of parked cars. Hold your line. You then remain *in* the traffic stream, where following traffic can see you.

Changing lanes

Treat each lane as a right turn, taking them one by one, with the difference that you don't wait in the middle by the white line. Your place when you're riding along a lane is the same as on a normal road: a yard or so from the left. Go from this position in one lane to that position in the other by the safest direct route, using the techniques in 'right turns'.

Keep an eye out for the traffic in the lane ahead of you when changing lanes to avoid running into it.

Roundabouts

If you're turning left, signal left and stay left. If not, it's better to head for the middle. When you pass the exit before the one you're taking, signal left and come across the roundabout carefully and directly. You may feel exposed, but traffic can at least see you. If you start from a position on the left (and don't turn left immediately) you risk being hit by traffic leaving the roundabout at any exit you're passing.

If you don't feel safe doing this, dismount, get on the footpath, and walk your bike around the roundabout.

Braking

When you brake, your weight is thrown forward. If you have to brake suddenly, push your weight back with your arms. Apply both brakes firmly. Don't snatch at them, particularly the rear, or you may go into an uncontrolled skid. Your front brake does most of your decelerating.

Obstacles

You're riding along with traffic behind you and you spot a pot-hole. What do you do? If you swerve you could get run over. Don't. Rise up on your pedals, with your knees loose, and let the bike flow over the pot-hole. If you can bunny-hop, jump it.

Practise bunny-hopping away from traffic. Squat down over the bike, then leap up, still holding onto the bars and keeping your feet on the pedals. Try it while riding along. Mountain bike magazines regularly teach this trick.

Above, left: If there's oncoming traffic, stop in the centre of the road just left of the white line. You have priority over traffic turning right from the side road, though drivers may not know this.

Above, right: If you're approaching a roundabout and want to turn right, you'll need to change lanes. Again, look back early.

Above: Hold your position to the right of the road on the roundabout entrance. Signal early, check over your shoulder and make for your exit.

Cycle safety means, first and foremost, being seen. If you ride round in black clothes at night you'll get run over.

CYCLE SAFETY

Cycling is not inherently dangerous. Cars are. They account for 95% of cycling fatalities and the vast majority of serious injuries among cyclists. In the majority of accidents involving adult cyclists, it's usually the car driver's fault.

Hone your own road skills and you're a lot less likely to be hit. Ride where you can be seen. Understand the mentality of the average motorist: he's not out to get you, he's just a bit stressed and drowsy from being cooped up in his car, and he's in sole charge of a blundering metal behemoth. You *must* register in his field of vision.

Visibility

During daylight hours, your position on the road and the obviousness of your manoeuvres are crucial. It's also worth dressing to be seen. Many cycling jerseys and jackets are day-glow yellow. They are garish, but you cannot miss them. That's the point.

At night-time, colours aren't really relevant. You need reflectives. Pedal reflectors and ankle-bands are excellent, as the up-down motion is eye-catching and immediately says 'cyclist'. A Sam Browne belt or a reflective vest is a must too. Wear one.

Lights

Bicycle lights traditionally showed other traffic where you were, but didn't show *you* where you were going. Not any more.

Cycle paths

Cycle paths in the UK are a great idea for many reasons. Sustrans are building a 6,500-mile network of paths for the millennium, often utilizing disused railways or towpaths. Since these old routeways go through the country and connect urban areas, they are great for touring and commuting as well as providing a car-free environment for leisure cyclists.

Not all paths are great, however. Some local councils have made token gestures and created routes that are unlit, littered with broken glass and dog mess, and that end suddenly, pitching you right into a busy road. Rememeber that you are not obliged to use such paths (or any cycle paths).

Reflectives prevent accidents. Helmets can save you from serious head injuries if you do have an accident.

Helmets

Helmets polarize opinions among cyclists: some love them, some hate them. You owe it to yourself to at least try one.

The reason some cyclists don't like helmets is that they treat the symptom of road danger, not the cause, and according to a frequently quoted statistic, you're more likely to suffer a head injury by falling down stairs or crashing your car. These statements are true, but it's your head.

For some forms of racing it is compulsory to wear a helmet, and it definitely makes sense to wear one for any kind of mountain biking. If you're touring on quiet lanes a helmet is less critical.

Children are advised to use helmets. The British Medical Association notes[1] that children are more likely to have the kind of accident in which helmets are of greatest benefit, i.e. those with no other vehicle involved.

If you decide to use a helmet some or all of the time, get one with a recognized safety standard (Snell, ANSI or BSI). Get one that fits comfortably and doesn't move about on your head; try before you buy. And don't get one that looks too 'nerdy', or you won't wear it. Weight and ventilation are the other criteria.

Footnote
1. *Cycling Towards Health and Safety*, **British Medical Association, 1992**

Systems like the Nightsun and BLT light up the whole road. They run off a rechargeable battery that fits in your bottle cage, and gives 1–6 hours light per charge. Twin lamps effectively give you 'dipped' and 'full beam'. You can even ride offroad at night with these lights. Naturally, they are not cheap: the Nightsun can cost in excess of £200.

On a budget, you're probably better off with a bottle dynamo like the AXA linked to a halogen front lamp. For occasional urban journeys, battery lights are fine. Be sure they fit securely.

At the rear of the bike, LED lights have no competition. They give excellent battery life (often over 100 hours) and are very visible. Flashing lights are easiest to see from behind, but the law in the UK says you must use a continuous light on your bike. Get two LED lights and set one to flash mode.

Above, left: LED rear lights are highly visible, and the batteries last for ages.

Left: If you want to see where you're going on unlit roads, get a rechargeable system like this one. It'll light up the whole road.

SUMMER RIDING GEAR

Cycling gear used to consist of woollen shorts, jerseys and a pair of flat black shoes. It looked, and was, solidly utilitarian. These days, however, cycling gear is more fashionable, but still as practical as ever.

Head

Your helmet must have adequate ventilation or on a hot day your head will poach. Buy one with plenty of vents – eight or more, though the size and position is obviously important too. The Giro Ventoux is a good benchmark. Some helmets come with a brow sweat pad.

If you don't wear a helmet, you should use a cycling cap to keep the sun off your head. Wear it reversed to keep the sun off your neck.

Normal clothing has seams in uncomfortable places, and is often too thick, too flappy, too floppy (shoes), or just too hot to cycle in.

If you plan to ride more than a few miles, it pays to wear the right gear. Padded shorts are crucial, and this top won't get wet and clammy like a cotton shirt. Stiff shoes stop your feet aching, and glasses keep grit, sun and insects out of your eyes.

Staying hydrated

If you're going to be cycling for an hour or more, take a full water bottle with you – the large, one-litre kind. Start drinking before you feel thirsty. If you're riding on a really hot day you may need as much as a litre an hour. If you're going for a long ride, take two bottles.

Mountain bikers tend to get water bottles covered with mud or dust, and have trouble reaching for them on rough terrain. A CamelBak is a better option. This is a flattish bladder of water with a long drinking tube, which is carried on your back like a rucksack. Some rucksacks have integral CamelBaks included.

Eyes

Sunglasses stop you squinting and serve as a barrier against wind, insects and dust. Standard ones don't wrap around to protect your eyes from the wind. If this doesn't bother you, you could use a cheap pair. Dedicated cycling glasses are better, but can be expensive. Use a neck cord to keep your glasses safe in case they slip off. Buy one from an opticians or rig something up yourself.

Hands

Fingerless cycling mitts provide good shock-absorbent padding for your hands and some protection for your palms in the event of a spill. Those with a towelling patch on the thumb are useful for mopping sweat.

Body

Cotton T-shirts get soggy with sweat. A cycling shirt with a Lycra/polyester mix will be quicker drying and better at keeping the breeze off you (because of its tighter fit). It will also have two or three pockets in the back, which are useful for carrying snacks or spares.

Take a wind-proof and shower-proof jacket on all but the shortest of rides. A cagoule is cheap; a Pertex jacket is best. It will weigh next to nothing and will pack down to fit in a seat pack or bum bag.

Legs

Padded shorts should be the first item of kit in your cycling wardrobe. They are *comfortable*. If you don't like Lycra you can get normal-looking shorts with inserts, or you could wear your cycling shorts beneath some baggy ones. Never ride any distance in clothing with thick seams (i.e. jeans).

Traditional shorts have a chamois (leather) insert, which needs to be kept supple with a special cream after washing. Synthetic pads are now pretty good, and are easier to live with. Eight-panel shorts give a better fit than six, and shorts made from a Coolmax/Lycra mix are less sweaty than those with a nylon/Lycra mix.

Leg-grippers at the ends of the shorts stop them riding up. Women's shorts are available with the seams in a different place.

Feet

Footwear needs to have a stiff sole to prevent your feet aching and to transfer your power most efficiently. Socks (without thick seams) help prevent blisters.

For any kind of racing, on or off-road, clipless pedals are *de rigeur*. Primarily they prevent your feet from slipping off the pedals, but in theory they also allow you to pedal through more of the crank's rotation.

Mountain bikers and tourers are advised to use SPD (Shimano Pedalling Dynamics)-compatible shoes, as the recessed cleat makes walking easier. Road racers tend to use a protruding cleat, since they don't need to get off the bike to run like mountain bikers or sight-see as tourists are likely to do.

Flat pedals and toe-clips are better for a utility bike, and some tourers prefer them, since you can then ride the bike wearing any shoes.

WINTER RIDING GEAR

Riding your bike in winter doesn't have to be unpleasant, but it will almost certainly be if you go out in the wrong kit. Properly togged up you can be warm, dry, and invigorated even in the worst weather.

Head

Winter is the time when you most need a helmet, as you're more likely to slip off your bike on ice or a wet drain cover and crack your head.

A well-ventilated helmet will not keep your head warm. You could get a less well ventilated helmet for winter use. Or you could wear a motorcyclist's silk balaclava underneath your helmet. Some hats will fit under a helmet too. Headbands that cover your ears are also good.

A peaked hat or peaked balaclava is excellent for keeping stinging rain or sleet out of your face; get one that also keeps your ears warm. If your jacket has a hood, make sure it doesn't obscure your vision – many do.

Hands and arms

Fleecy-lined neoprene or Gore-Tex gloves will keep your hands warm and dry. When it's really cold, wear silk glove liners too, or use Gore-Tex covered mittens (mittens are warmer than gloves). For short, occasional journeys, the cheapest option is to wear thick woollen gloves inside washing-up gloves. On longer rides these quickly become damp with sweat.

The arms of your jacket must be long enough so that there's no gap between jacket and glove. Elasticated or Velcro cuffs prevent water or cold air entering. Use arm warmers when it's really cold.

Body

When dressing use the layering principle, explained below: a wicking layer, an insulating layer and an outer layer.

Make sure your jacket is long enough in the back, and has a drawstring closure at hem and throat, otherwise it'll scoop up cold air. A scarf can make a big difference and is easy to add or remove. Jacket zips should be covered by wide

flaps, and the seams should be sealed for maximum waterproofing.

There are lots of Gore-Tex jackets around. Be sure to get one that's designed for cycling. Traditional rain capes, which keep your lower body dry by looping over your thumbs, are still made by Carradice. Unless it's very windy, these are great for utility cycling, and they're cheap too.

Legs

Wear thick cycling tights over your shorts; Cannondale and Bouré make good ones. If it's

This jacket is long enough in the arm, but isn't so long in the body that it'll catch on the saddle. The head, hands and feet are well protected too.

So long as you're moving you're generating heat, and will need less wrapping up than if standing around. But you may have to make an unscheduled stop so keep a layer or two in reserve.

really cold, wear leg warmers to keep your knees warm. Bouré's are good. Use bib tights to stop your lower back getting cold, or fit braces to your cycling tights.

For rain protection, it's Gore-Tex again – overtrousers this time. Get ones with tabs that can be fastened to stop flapping at the ankles. Spats work well with a cycling cape.

Feet

Overshoes, often neoprene, are essential if you wear standard cycling shoes. They're not generally 100% waterproof, especially if you've got waterproof trousers on, as these act like drainpipes to your ankles.

Gore-Tex socks are your last line of defence, these really will keep your feet dry and warm. They are expensive but worth it.

The layering principle

On a bike your body temperature can vary a lot. Uphill you generate a lot of heat, and sweat; downhill you get chilled by the wind. You get too hot or too cold. Wear several thin layers rather than one thick one as you can always remove layers or replace them as appropriate.

Next to your skin, your base layer, you should wear a lightweight garment that wicks away sweat – a thermal vest, perhaps. Above that you need one or two insulating layers, such as a cycling shirt and a fleece or woollen jumper. And above that, you need a water-proof and wind-proof layer, such as a Gore-Tex jacket. This outer layer, like the others, should be breathable.

You will often find that you need to remove a layer after you've been cycling for a while, as you generate a lot of heat riding.

JARGON BUSTER

Coolmax
Man-made fabric that's useful for wicking away sweat, and works well next to the skin.

Gore-Tex
A layered material that's breathable, waterproof and windproof. It's made up of a membrane – the Gore-Tex itself – which is porous to water as vapour (sweat) but not as liquid (rain), and which is sandwiched between a nylon or polyester outer and a loose, airy inner.

Neoprene
Slightly stretchy material that stays warm when wet. Used in wetsuits. Some overshoes are made from Neoprene.

Pertex
Soft, durable fabric made of tightly woven, super-fine nylon yarns. It compacts well, is breathable, windproof and reasonably water resistant – though not as water resistant as Gore-Tex.

Roubaix
Generic name for any tights, leg warmers or arm warmers that are thicker than the standard Lycra/Coolmax garments and have a fleecy-lining. The main material will typically be a Lycra/nylon or Lycra/polyester mix.

DON'T LEAVE HOME WITHOUT IT

Motorists used to have a road safety slogan drummed into them: 'Clunk-click, every trip'. Cyclists should memorize their own mantra: 'Pack spares, every trip'. Even the shortest journey can be marred by a puncture. Why walk when you can repair or replace?

On every journey a bike should carry the following:
> pump
> puncture repair kit (or self-stick patches)
> spare inner tube
> basic tool kit

Less essential but always handy is some small change for an emergency chocolate bar or phone call. Pack everything into a small saddle pack or bottle cage holder, something that you can easily take off the bike so it won't get stolen.

Extended touring

Pack too much and the severe weight penalties will spoil your trip. Pack too little and you may find that you have a long walk to civilization.

Instead of packing spare parts for your oil-filled suspension forks you should think about fitting a pair less prone to failing in the first place. Think simple. The more moving parts a component has and the more fiddly it is to get inside them, the more chance they will be unfixable en route. Choose a bike and components which can be easily maintained.

Essential touring tools:

Spare tyre; chain lube; grease and extra bearings; extra chain links; spare cables; Hex spanners; spare spokes; pedal removal tool; cone spanners; freewheel removal tool; bottom bracket tools.

TIP

> Check your spare tube often. Make sure your spare tube has a valve which will fit your rims (a Shraeder valve may not fit in some rims designed for Presta valves, for instance) and that it is a new or repaired one rather than the punctured tube you meant to replace last trip!

Tools

Bicycles are low-tech items and even when complicated parts fail it's simple to rig up repairs that will get you to your eventual destination. The worst that can normally happen is that your bodged repairs are ugly, unsafe for long term use and a bit of a pain because they rattle, hum and have to be redone every half an hour or so. Pedalling a mashed 21-speed gear ensemble converted into a single speed make-do may be annoying but it's better than being completely stranded in the back of beyond.

Above: Zip ties can fix almost anything to anything.

Left: The Cool-Tool is a marvel of miniaturisation, but the Allen keys are prone to going missing.

A judicious selection of tools will allow you to handle most roadside repairs. The bare essentials include a small adjustable spanner; 4, 5, and 6mm Allen keys (or Allen key cluster); tyre levers; a small screwdriver and a chain-breaking tool. There are also many combination tools, some of them surprisingly compact and effective. The best known is the Cool-Tool, which is adjustable spanner and chain-breaking tool with Allen keys attached. The Leatherman (knife, screwdriver, and pliers) is also useful.

Don't scrimp on tools; get a quality set for reliability. It's no good carrying spare tools around for months if they're going to break the first time you use them.

Night-time riding

If you're going to be out at night don't forget to pack lights and clothing with reflective finishes. A trade-name to look out for on many cycle garments is Reflec: this is an ink made with microscopic glass beads which, when printed onto shorts, jackets and leggings, acts like a covering of millions of cats-eyes. Clothing fully printed with Reflec ink lights up the whole of your body-shape.

The ink can be made in any colour so garments are available which light up at night yet look like normal printed designs in the day. A black jacket printed all-over with a black Reflec ink will appear as black in the daylight but flare up as bright silver under headlights.

FAMILY CYCLING

Children enjoy cycling from an early age, but until they're capable of riding for several miles under their own steam you'll need some kind of carrying or towing device.

Above: When they're able to sit unaided, babies are ready for child-seats. Their weight will affect how the bike handles, particularly if the bike has a step-through frame. Use a mountain bike or hybrid instead.

Child trailers

A trailer is a kind of two-wheeled caravan for children, which attaches by an articulated fixing to the left-hand chain stay or the seat post of the towing bike. Most seat two children, up to the ages or five or six. Children as young as six weeks can ride in a trailer if they are firmly strapped in in a carrycot or child's car seat.

Trailers offer many advantages: you can carry two children, who are protected from the elements; your bike handling is unaffected, unlike with child seats; and you can carry groceries as well as, or instead of, the children. Many fold down, so you don't need a garage.

Trailers are safer than they look. Most come with bright safety flags, but are very visible on their own. Heads turn at 200 yards (180m

approx), and cars give a wide berth. The articulated fixing means that the trailer stays upright even if the towing bike falls over, while the children are secured with waist and shoulder belts.

Child seats

Front seats fix to the top tube, rear ones behind the adult's saddle, either to an existing rack or a purpose-built rack. Children can go into either when they can sit up properly – usually between seven and nine months.

Front ones affect bike-handling less, and your child is cradled between your arms, but the small-seat-and-footrest kind are only suitable for older children; say four years and up. Tinies are better off strapped into fully supported front seats that look like smaller versions of rear seats. Such seats generally fit children up to about the age of two-and-a-half years old.

Rear seats will suit children up to about 40lb (18kg approx) in weight; more than this and the handling of the bike will suffer. Choose a seat that has support for the child's head, straps for feet (to keep them out of the spokes) and shoulder *and* waist straps. The rack and seat should be rigid. If you use a sprung saddle, beware trapped fingers.

Children will often fall asleep in child seats and droop forward, so be sure straps offer full support. A bootlace through a helmet vent and tied to the back of the seat can help keep them in an upright position. Never leave a child unattended in a child seat.

Trailer cycles

A trailer cycle is essentially half a bicycle that bolts to the adult's bike, creating an articulated tandem. Some bolt to a special rack, others to the seat post.

Trailer cycles suit children aged between four and ten, though the child shouldn't be more than half as heavy as the adult. Always use mudguards on the towing bike to prevent road debris hitting the child. Fit toe-clips to the trailer bike to prevent flailing legs.

Brakes are not fitted to trailer bikes, though gears often are. These allow the child to contribute more. Two-seater trailer cycles are available with two rear wheels. Single wheel versions will not carry luggage.

Tandems

A tandem is a great family vehicle. It can be equipped with child seats, or tow a trailer or trailer cycle, and it can be adapted for use by one adult and a child.

Kiddy cranks are a bolt-on chainset and bottom bracket that fits part way up the rear seat tube. They connect to the drive system via an extra chain. Children from three years and up can use kiddy cranks, which can be lowered and then removed as the child grows.

Fit wrap-around bars for younger children. These are two sets of inverted dropped bars with lengths of tubing positioned between them.

Although tandems exist designed for one adult and one child, it's not expensive to adapt an adult tandem with kiddy cranks.

CYCLING FOR CHILDREN

From the age of three and upwards, children can learn to ride their own bike. They'll find cycling a lot easier if the bike isn't overweight and cheaply constructed, as many junior bikes are.

The bike

Children's bikes are smaller than adults' bikes but are not that much easier or quicker for a manufacturer to make. The only way for them to push the price down is to use cheaper materials and less exacting procedures. Which is why so many are so awful. Too much weight – children's frames often weigh more than an adult's – plastic bearings, and worthless brakes are just a few of the common problems.

A good bike will cost more, but can be handed down or re-sold whereas a cheap one will end up in the bin. And a light bike with proper bearings, and decent, child-sized components is so much easier and considerably more pleasant for a child to ride. Young children aren't strong enough to ride real clunkers.

The first bike should be small enough for the child to put both feet flat when the saddle is at its lowest (see below Learning to ride). Avoid the temptation to buy a bike with 'growing room'; it's not a jumper or a coat.

Handlebars should be narrow enough that the child's arms aren't splayed out, and shouldn't be so far forward that the rider has to lean too far over; most children like to cycle fairly upright. Saw down the bars and fit a new stem if necessary. Don't use dropped bars until your child is seven or eight years old.

One gear is plenty to start with; six or twelve only confuse. For a second bike (or an upgraded first) a three-speed hub gear is nice and simple. Derailleurs can wait till later. Be advised that chain stays need to be about 15.5 inches (40cm approx) or more for derailleurs to work properly.

Children must be able to reach their brake levers. If they can't and the levers on the bike aren't adjustable, you can fit adult two-finger MTB levers, which are.

Do not buy a bike with plastic bearing in the hubs, bottom bracket or headset. Toy shops often sell such bikes.

Avoid gimmicks like suspension forks; on a child's bike they are likely to be low quality and useless. But do let your child personalise their bike. It's their bike, after all. They'll like using their bell, drinking from their water bottle and so on.

The best way to get your child riding is to put the saddle right down and remove the pedals. Your child uses the bike as a scooter, and learns to balance.

Learning to ride

Stabilizers belong in the bin. They don't do any harm, but your child won't learn to balance and ride a bike until they're removed. So they're effectively useless. Instead, remove the pedals. The right-hand pedal unscrews clockwise, the left-hand pedal anticlockwise. Then lower the saddle so that your child can rest both feet on the floor and push himself along.

Let the child scoot around like this for an afternoon or two, to get the hang of steering and braking. As they get used to it, encourage them to scoot with both feet at the same time, momentarily taking their feet off the floor and allowing them to freewheel. This will help them to get a sense of balance.

Cranks for kids

Cranks on many children's bikes are too long. As with adults, they should be about ⅕ of the inside leg.

Inside leg (cm)	Crank length (mm)
40–45	90
46–50	100
51–55	110
56–60	120
61–65	130
66–70	140

Cranks can be shortened by some cycle specialists.

Then re-fit the pedals and let him go. Don't hold the back of the saddle and run along. It'll hurt you and make your child anxious, provoking a panic attack and fall when you do let go. As the child gets used to riding, gradually raise the saddle, and show them how to get off it when stopping.

Children are the one group of cyclists who regularly fall off a bike and bang their head. Make sure they use a helmet.

If cranks are too long children find pedalling very hard. Don't be tempted to use stablizers; they just delay the learning process.

When locking your bike up, you should secure the wheels and fill the shackle of the lock with as much bike or street furniture as possible.

BIKE SECURITY

To the urban thief an unlocked bike is as big a gift as a dropped wallet. Even a U-lock may only slow him down by six seconds; we've timed a professional lock-breaker tackling one. But U-locks are found to be effective against casual thieves.

Your bike

If it looks attractive it will get stolen. 'Attractive' means a mountain bike, especially an expensive mountain bike. If you must commute on a £1,000 Cannondale, do not leave it outside. Ever. Bring it in, then lock it to something – like your ankle.

Some cycle couriers try to disguise their expensive mountain bikes by wrapping black tape or foam padding around the main tubes. This will put off opportunists. Most cycle couriers ride bikes that, though very functional, really *are* as cheap as they look. This is a good idea. The cheaper and more like a utility bike it looks, the less likely your bike is to get stolen.

When you lock your bike, do not lock it down

Many locks can be snipped open in seconds with a big pair of bolt cutters. Use an expensive U-lock – it'll cost less than a new bike.

an alley. Lock it where it's in plain view of a lot of people. And *always* lock it, until it boooomeo habit. It takes less time for someone to steal an unlocked bike than it does for you to rush out the shop whose window you left it against, thinking it was safely in sight.

Your lock

All locks can be breached, but the best U-locks will only fall to an angle grinder or 20 minutes of hammering, levering and smashing with a BIG pry bar…and either method would attract attention to a thief.

Top locks include the Trelock Titan, Kryptonite New York and Squire Paramount. U-locks are available at half, or even a third, of the price of these brands. Do not buy them. They are worse than useless, because they give you a false sense of security.

When locking your bike, attach it to a solid object like some iron railings. Leave as little space as possible in the U of the lock. Remove your front wheel, place it against the railings, and then pass the U-lock through your seat or chain stays, both wheels, and the railings. If you have a quick release saddle and seat post, take it with you.

Don't lock your bike to a post if it can be lifted over the top. Even if it can't, be aware that some thieves have been known to saw the tops off parking meters etc and then replace them so they can swipe bikes later.

Finally, do not leave easily removable accessories, like panniers or lights, on your bike – they *will* be stolen. And do not leave bikes unlocked on a car rack.

Home security

Keep your bike locked up at home. It's not enough for it to be behind a locked garage or shed door; outbuildings are easy to break into. Put an expander bolt or two into a brick wall and lock your bike to them – it really is worth it.

Alternatively, get a pickaxe, make a hole in a concrete floor, put the end of a big chain in the hole, and fill with concrete. Lock your bike to the chain. Big chains can be obtained from scrap metal merchants; boat mooring rings are good too.

Consider fitting an alarm to your shed or garage. An automatic light with an infra-red sensor is handy too. These are cheaper than you think and are effective deterrents.

Insurance

Increasing rates of theft have made premiums for bike insurance soar. Some insurers will simply not insure a bike in the worst hit urban areas. Most insurers have lowered their 'maximum value insured' level.

Shop around, and read the small print. Many household contents insurers will insure bikes as part of the package, but the limit on value is likely to be too low. The cover may only be valid when the bike is at home too.

Cycling organizations can usually arrange insurance for their members. Rates are often pretty high, but the sky is the limit for value. Some do a 'no claims' bonus, and discounts for multiple bikes.

Given a choice between breaking into a garage with an alarm and a garage without, few thieves will pick the former.

If all this talk of security makes you feel paranoid – good. If you are worried about having your bike stolen it is far less likely to happen.

TRANSPORTING YOUR BIKE

In the general run of things bikes are neither heavy nor bulky. They can be taken apart and fitted into pretty small spaces. Even when kept whole they can be stored with ease by aircraft, ferries and trains, although persuasion is often needed to make carriers understand this.

By car

If dismantling and storing inside isn't an option there are many exterior racks available – some very cheap (and nasty) others high quality and expensive. Tow ball racks and the Thule rooftop systems are the strongest but those which affix to the windows of hatchbacks are good enough to hold two bikes with no problems. Affix bikes to racks with toe-straps and nylon webbing with non-slip buckles rather than bungee cords – they're more secure and less likely to damage you or your bike. An extra number plate is a legal requirement when transporting rear-mounted bikes in the UK.

On the train

In the UK, getting bikes on trains can be a problem and it's a bone of contention between

Left: An additional number plate isn't just an expensive accessory for your boot-mounted bike rack, it's a legal requirement.

cyclists and the railways. Since British Rail was sold off, the restrictions on InterCity services have stayed in place – bikes must be booked on in advance, cost £3 each with a maximum of three bikes per train – but they may be relaxed in the future.

The French rail system, SNCF (Société Nationale des Chemins de Fer) is one of the largest and best in Europe and is fairly bike friendly. Its rules are similar to those of other European countries and what applies in France can be considered the norm across most of Europe. You can take your bike with you as baggage at no charge on around 2000 trains daily. These trains are indicated with a bicycle symbol on the schedules posted in the train stations. You are responsible for loading and unloading your bike yourself.

On trains where it is not possible to take your bike as hand baggage (most long distance routes on the high-speed TGV) it will be necessary to register the bike as unaccompanied baggage. Take your bike to the 'baggages' counter at the train station a good half an hour prior to the train's departure. Loading and unloading is done by the SNCF staff but your bike doesn't always travel with you on the same train. At best you can expect to claim your bike the next day. On international routes, there can be a delay of several days.

By air

Bikes and luggage within the 44lb (20kg) allowance travel free on airlines. It's best to leave your bike looking like a bike. In a box baggage handlers don't treat it as carefully.

Ride, fully packed, to the airport. Once in the departure terminal let the pressure out of the tyres, take water bottle cages off and turn the handlebars to the side so the bike is not so wide. All the heavy weights and all the panniers, bar one, get left on the bike. The bags help protect the gears and the wheels when being stowed. Make sure the panniers stay put by clamping them on with reusable zip-ties.

Use the poly-bags provided by airlines to wrap your bike (this protects both the bike and other people's luggage). Don't use cardboard bike-boxes as they offer little protection. Airport baggage handlers throw anonymous boxes of all sizes and types in the hold and load suitcases on top. Bikes get lifted gently into the hold and generally get placed in a secure position where they won't cause damage.

By ferry

Bikes are normally carried free on ferries and as they can be rolled on and off quite easily they do not need to be packaged in boxes. Lock them to rails, however, otherwise they might wander around the hold due to the rocking and the rolling of the ferry.

Protecting your bike in a padded bag isn't always necessary but can help if you need to pack the bike in as small a space as possible.

```
TIP
> If airline staff refuse to carry your bike
unless it's boxed, consider volunteering to
sign the disclaimer panel on your ticket.
This means the airline is not liable for any
damage. This may seem cavalier on your part
but bikes kept as bikes suffer less damage
than bikes in anonymous boxes.
```

OFF ROAD RIDING

STARTING OFF

From flat canal tow-path rides to scaling Scottish peaks, mountain biking is all about exploration. And it's exploration far out of the reach of the dreaded motorcar. There are plenty of people who get their kicks from riding among traffic but mountain bikers prefer the fresh air and wide open spaces of the hills and dales.

Mountain biking is becoming just another way to enjoy the countryside – no longer is it solely the domain of begoggled teenagers, now people of all ages and abilities get out on bikes. Mountain biking can be done by those who feel the need to cycle 75 miles before breakfast, or it can be enjoyed by families doing an 11-mile gentle pedal around beautiful landscaped parks prettified by the Forestry Commission.

The hills are alive with the sound of...mountain bikers having fun. Fat tyres spell off-road freedom.

Why the mountain bike?

The better safety and stability, durability, low maintenance and go-almost-anywhere capability of the mountain bike makes it an ideal choice for the casual leisure rider.

Of course, MTBs cannot go everywhere, there are plenty of places where mountain biking is completely impractical and where feet win hands down but for forest trails, wide tracks, estate roads, bridleways and other linear routes the mountain bike really does come into its own.

More for your money

Whatever type and brand of mountain bike you go for, it will cost upwards of £300 if you want it to be reliable and last. All bikes may look alike but they differ significantly. Basically, spending more gets you:

> lighter weight
> a more lively, responsive frame
▶ more precise gear shifting, braking and handling
> longer lasting, more serviceable componentary.

Test ride bikes in various price ranges to decide whether, in your opinion, the improved performance justifies the cost. Don't scrimp and save, though, mountain bikes are not toys. Bargain basement bikes-in-boxes are not cut out for off-road cycling.

Where to buy

Specialist cycle dealers don't only make a living selling bikes, they offer a service too. A good dealer is worth his mark-up because of expert advice and after-sales support. Supermarkets and discount warehouses offer cheap bikes but ask yourself how they can do this. It's not all economies of scale; it's also by saving on things such as zero post-purchase care.

Off road riding puts strain on your bike – cheap components will not be up to the job.

Sizing up

MTBs need a smaller frame for a given leg length than road bikes. A typical size is 13 inches shorter than your inside leg. Mountain bikes fit better with 5–6 inches of seat post out of the frame.

Things to look for

A good bike starting at around £300 will have a lightweight chromoly steel frame, probably mass-produced in Taiwan. Extremely knobbly fat tyres are a must for muddy conditions but many entry level bikes will compromise with less knobbly tyres which are suitable for both tarmac and the dirt. If you plan to do most of your riding on flat, railway paths then these type of tyres are fine, otherwise fit knobbly ones, they give more traction off-road.

> ## TIP
>
> Only buy from those bike shops which let you ride the machines before you purchase. It's important to ride many bikes before you choose one you feel truly comfortable on.

Types of Mountain Bike

Entry level off-road bikes

Bikes in this category will weigh 30lbs and upwards. Tyres, saddles and pedals are likely to be basic and may need to be upgraded soon after purchase. Do not buy a bike fitted with suspension at this price level (£300) – the bouncy forks will be poor imitations of the forks on more expensive bikes.

Race bikes

This is where real quality starts. You can expect lots of extras on bikes at this price range (£500–£800), including good quality tyres. Suspension forks are common, although standard forks are also available. Exotic frame materials such as titanium and aluminium start to appear.

Dream bikes

This is the realm of off-the-peg dream bikes, and custom built machines. Exotic materials are common. A good titanium bike with titanium components for lightness and many extras can easily cost £2000.

Suspension

Some bikes now come fitted with front and rear suspension. Unless you'll be doing lots of crazy downhilling such bounciness is overkill. However, if you suffer discomfort in the wrists, arms and shoulders a pair of front suspension forks will be a godsend.

OFF ROAD KIT

Clothing

Mountain biking is a very energetic activity, one which rapidly warms you up. This is why many cycle-specific jackets made from so-called 'breathable' materials have vents all over the place – without cool air coming into the jacket a cyclist stews in his or her own juices within ten minutes of moderate to hard pedalling even in quite cold conditions. Mountain bikers need to layer-up, but they need the thinnest of layers and only a very thin outer shell.

If you head for the wilds, don't rely on a T-shirt to keep you comfy. In every condition but a heatwave, cotton is useless.

Key features – MTB jacket

> Short at front – to prevent bunching up on the stomach when crouched over in the riding position
> Very long at rear – to stop the jacket riding up; to protect the kidneys from wind; to keep the backside as dry as possible in rain
> Wide shoulders and long arms – to give protection, even when riding in a stretched out position
> Vents – to help with air circulation, to prevent heat build-up and to release sweat
> High collar, with effective neck closures – to protect the neck from wind and to stop wind billowing out the jacket whilst cycling

Key features – MTB jersey

> Man-made fabrics – to wick moisture from skin
> Stand-up collar and neck zipper – to seal in body heat, while allowing it to be undone for ventilation control
> Shoulders cut wider – for comfort even when arms positioned forward
> Sleeves shaped for forward lean position
> Pockets at rear – to carry energy food

> Tight and form-fitted – to reduce flapping and binding
> Cut longer in back – to accommodate forward lean

Key features – MTB shorts (skin-tight)

> Stretchy material – for freedom of motion
> Sometimes two layers of fabric – for added crash protection
> Multi-panel construction – for form-fitting comfort
> Lower cut front – so that abdomen not constricted
> Smooth, soft saddle pad – to minimize friction and cushion bumps
> Long legs – to prevent saddle chafing
> Elasticated leg grippers – to hold shorts in place on thigh

TIP

> To prevent saddle chafing, cycle shorts are worn without underwear. A 'Visible Pantie Line' is a sure sign of a novice cyclist!

Legwear

Shorts are good for races and for summer but tights are more practical year-round. Fleece-backed ones, available from Karrimor and others, offer cold weather and crash protection. Leg warmers are useful if the weather is changeable.

If you decide to ride with cycle shorts, buy the best. Cheap Lycra shorts have a tendency to split at inopportune moments. Eight-panel shorts are expensive but tough, protective and last a very long time.

Footwear

In the good old days mountain bikers getting out onto the hills used their heavy leather walking boots. Nowadays they favour either lightweight fabric boots (usually with sole-attachments for clicking into the small clipless pedals favoured by enthusiasts), or expensive race-type shoes with stiff soles. These help improve pedalling efficiecy because less energy is spent flexing floppy soles. They are usually held onto the pedal by toe-clips and straps.

SPD pedals and the shoes to go with them have definite advantages over boots and toe-clips. You're connected to the bike for a start. The SPD system is easy to learn and well worth it for both bike handling reasons and pedalling efficiency.

Clipless pedals are secure and improvo pedalling efficiency.

Helmet

As mountain biking carries a higher likelihood of crashing than road cycling it makes sense to protect your head. Helmets are almost uniform wear amongst mountain bikers, much more so than for road cyclists. Look out for standards such as Snell and ANSI.

If you get serious about downhilling, light-weight full-face helmets are recommended to protect your head and face. They are expensive but you will be glad you bought one if you have a mother-of-all-crashes.

Mitts

Padded cycle gloves are excellent for road cycling but vital for mountain biking. Again it's because taking a tumble is part and parcel of life away from the tarmac. Falling onto grass is no problem but sliding along a gravel dirt track deposits a lot of skin. Always ride in mitts.

If you're riding in the wilds, take plenty of fluid with you. CamelBaks, as worn by these two cyclists, are an excellent way to carry much needed drinks.

WOMEN'S SHORTS

Cycle shorts are designed with men in mind so women do well to invest in specific women's shorts. These cost more but are superior in fit and comfort. The padding is in a more woman-friendly position and the cut of the shorts is more suited to woman's different frame.

TRAIL SKILLS

The traditional method of learning basic mountain biking skills is by trial and error, although some outdoor activity centres – the Youth Hostel Association, for instance – offer introductory courses.

Controlled springs

There are two important concepts to grasp if you want to be both safe on the bike and able to manoeuvre correctly. First, your body must become a spring, and second, your weight distribution on the bicycle must be loose yet controlled. When riding over bumps, don't sit on the saddle soaking up all the punishment; hover an inch or two above the saddle using your inner thighs to lightly grip the nose of the saddle. Your arms should be bent and your posterior slightly off the back of the saddle. Your pedals must be perpendicular and your legs bent, acting as coiled springs. Don't straighten or stiffen your legs and arms – and don't clench the handlebars too tightly, keep relaxed and fluid. In this position you can control the bicycle downhill and over the roughest terrain.

Your centre of gravity should change depending on the severity of the bumps – if they're harsh, push your weight back. When using this technique for bumpy downhills keep both brakes on lightly to slow you down and keep you in control.

The key to effective climbing and downhilling is weight distribution. Lean forward to keep the front wheel on the ground for ascents and get your weight over the saddle for descents.

TIP

> Clenching your inner thighs over the nose of the saddle when descending is the way to 'feel' the bike over and around obstacles. But don't clamp too tightly – it's a light touch you're after not a vice-like grip.

GET ATTACHED TO YOUR BIKE

Try to graduate onto SPD clipless pedals as soon as you can. Once you're used to them they really do improve your bike-handling skills, especially jumping and avoiding obstacles.
Set them loosely to begin with so you know you can get out of them in a hurry but gradually increase the tension over time so your foot stays locked in place. With a positive wrench you'll still be able to 'clip-out' but the tightness will give you a great deal of control, especially compared to systems such as clips and toestraps, where feet can pop out during abrupt or difficult manoeuvres.

Bike skiing

Once you've mastered the coiled-spring downhill technique for bumpy ground, the bicycle should feel like a fluid object underneath you while remaining totally under your control. Downhill cycling becomes a bit like skiing; your body and weight does the steering as you lean into turns. The bicycle should be at one with your body.

This technique works equally well on tame descents, bumpy tracks and incredibly steep drop-offs. It is the most basic off-road riding stance and has many variations – new riders or those on reasonable ground do not have to take the position to extremes, simply remember to keep loose, fluid and springy!

Uphill technique

Uphill riding involves getting up out of the saddle when the gradient gets really steep, pushing hard with the legs and using the arms in a shallow rowing motion. You need to have your weight forward to keep the front wheel on the ground (if you sit going up steep hills you may 'wheelie' backwards) but not so far forward that the rear wheel loses traction. Keep balanced and alter your weight distribution as bumps come along.

Sit down if you have to get your breath back and drop a gear or two. Then, when you have recovered slightly, put the effort in once more. Hill climbing is tough on the lungs and legs but if you earn a good downhill, it's worth the effort.

Speed is the best way to make a splash for the camera but a slow, controlled crossing is often more effective.

TRAIL SKILLS FOR MTB TOURERS

Your first couple of hours on a loaded expedition mountain bike are critical. You must relearn how to steer, corner at speed and brake in a hurry. If touring is good for nothing else it's brilliant at making you appreciate your normal, unloaded bike.

Once you're up and running, the loaded expedition bike is smooth and stable – rock solid in fact, especially if you've packed it right. It's when you hit bumps or get out of the saddle that you realize your bike doesn't respond in the normal way.

Riding techniques

Cornering

It's difficult to change direction quickly with heavy panniers attached to your bike but corners can still be taken fast if you dare. On tarmac you can dip into corners at speed, so long as the weight distribution in your bags is correct. Pack the weighty items in the bottom of the bag – this keeps your centre of gravity low. Until you're used to the bike, anticipate corners in plenty of time and slow to the appropriate speed before you take them. Build up your cornering speed slowly and never forget you've got bags on – unlike a normal bike you've now got stuff to snag on obstacles.

Just like on a motorbike, your handlebars are not so much for steering as for holding onto: use your weight to 'lean' around the bend.

Brakes

Braking half way round a corner is fatal but stopping on a perfectly ordinary stretch of road can be dangerous too. The extra weight does funny things to your stopping distance. Think ahead. Your best brake is your front one. It is more efficient and, with a few weeks' supply of gear on the back of the bike, it's unlikely to toss you over the handle bars. The back brake is more likely to cause a skid and at high speeds with a heavy load may take the back wheel right out from under you.

TIP

> An overladen bike soon teaches you the importance of extreme packing ie if it's not essential don't pack it. An item that is chosen for 'just in case' reasons is a good candidate for dumping. You're over-loaded if your luggage weighs more than the bike.

Cadence

Your 'cadence' is your pedalling rate – ie the number of times your feet spin round while pedalling during a given time.

Road racers aim for 90-100 rotations per minute (rpm) but the average tourer can be satisfied with 75. Test your cadence by counting your rpm while travelling at a comfortable pace along a straight stretch of road or with a cycle computer if you have one that measures cadence. If you average less than 75, you'll be more effective in the next gear down. At first this may seem to use more energy than grinding away in a higher one, but in fact it's much more efficient and less tiring in the long term. Importantly, it's also less strain for the knees.

This rule of 75+ rotations a minute is even more important when going up hills or into headwinds when strains and tiredness are more likely, so change down gears accordingly.

Up hills

Go slow but sure. Keep a steady pace, think about something else and find fascination in roadside vegetation.

It's no failure to get off and walk but you'll usually find it's more difficult pushing a laden bike uphill than pedalling it. Instead of walking just take a breather every so often. Pretend you're looking at a map or take a swig of your water if you don't want passers-by to think you are fazed by the hill.

Some people stand on their pedals to 'honk' up a hill. It adds variation – and certainly relieves posterior pressure – but can be tiring and extremely unstable with panniers.

Down dale

After crawling to the top of the hill, there's a strong temptation to go crazy on the way down. It's up to you, and if the way ahead is straight and quiet it may be okay to do just that. But a heavy bike can easily shoot down a hill at 50mph, and a pot-hole, a blown tyre, or a stray animal wandering across the road can cause you to wipe-out in a major way.

Above: The most important skill for any tourer is navigation. Bar mounted map holders allow you to keep on the right road (or trail) without having to dig through your panniers and pockets to find a map.

Opposite page: It is possible to ride a loaded bike at a fast pace on a trail. The key is to load the bike correctly and watch out for obstacles.

ROUTE PLANNING

Even your favourite rides can become dull through repetition. Seeking pastures new is part of the joy of off-road riding. It's all about exploration and finding out what's around the next corner.

There are three basic ways of planning a ride:
1. Pick an area and randomly check out the trails.
2. Use a guide book to the area to choose the trails which best suit your mood and fitness level.
3. Buy a map of the area and work out which routes look good in theory.

You must remember that not all trails are open to mountain bikers. There are distinct zones to stick to. In the UK, bike access to footpaths, hill country and other areas is fairly complicated but there are specific areas, paths and tracks where cyclists can and cannot go.

Many good-looking routes are closed to mountain bikes but this need not be a problem – Europe is criss-crossed by a veritable maze of fantastic off-road routes that are completely legal to ride upon.

Footpaths

Technically speaking, where there is a public right of way anybody, including cyclists, has the right to use a footpath as a linear route. There is no tested criminal law against cycling on a footpath (except for those that run parallel to roads).

However, some local councils have prohibited all cyclists from footpaths. As the problem of bike access on footpaths is not clearly defined in law, mountain bikers often judge for themselves whether or not to cycle on them – discretion should be employed where necessary and both the rights of the landowner and the rights of fellow outdoor users must be taken into consideration. The characteristics of the path – is it wide enough for walkers and cyclists to pass in safety? Will it erode easily? Am I being a nuisance by using this path? – should be evaluated.

Bridleways

This type of highway is the one most legally accessible to cyclists. Biking members of the public have been granted the statutory right to ride their cycles on bridleways but they must give way to walkers and horse riders.

Tour Research

For wilderness expeditions there are two distinct schools of thought. One says plan like hell because you'll need to know all your options

Left: Two tourers look forward to a beautiful trail stretching out into the hills.

Right: Bridleways and cycle paths offer traffic-free riding in Europe. This one takes in a golf course.

Below: Not every good-looking trail is open to wheels. Footpaths, even wide, inviting ones are forbidden. Check an OS map for legality.

TIP

> No need to cycle across the hidden parts of the Gobi desert to find areas untouched by mass tourism, just pick a half-way exotic rural area – perhaps 50 miles or so away from tourist honey-pots – and start pedalling!

when things inevitably start to go wrong. And the other says don't do any studying because plans never work anyway. Either way, it's best to be flexible at all times. The Arabs say 'Insh'Allah', or 'as God wills it' – you need to develop just such a fatalistic attitude. What will be, will be.

If your original idea doesn't work out, the alternative may not be the end of the world. Normally it's the contrary. A couple of days spent stranded in a village hut by bad weather may not be on your schedule, but perhaps the villagers will introduce you to a unique side of local life. If you don't have an open mind and time to go off at a tangent you'll miss a great deal on your cycle tour.

Don't plan: research. Discover all the options. Read around your subject. But recognize that none of it will make sense or click into place until you arrive.

Pore over maps by all means (this is always a good part of any trip) but unless you can talk to somebody who's been to the area on a bike it's best to wait until you arrive before planning routes and schedules that may be physically possible but detract from an enjoyable, relaxed and absorbing trip.

EMERGENCIES

Crashes are a fact of mountain biking life. That's fine if you take a tumble a couple of miles from home and can limp back, but what about accidents miles from anywhere. It pays to take precautions of course, but even the best laid plans go wrong so you need a basic knowledge of first aid. For you and the bike. An injured bike can often be just as perilous as an injured biker.

The next best thing to having a doctor as a trail-mate is packing a first aid kit and knowing how to use it.

Emergency repairs:
Humans

You can either assemble your own first aid kit or buy one ready-to-go from outdoor shops (don't take the first aid kits given away by insurance companies and the like; these are home kits, and are not suitable for bike touring). For the extra expense of buying a full kit, you are guaranteed something compact and complete. Packs, such as the Gregson kit, are also watertight and have excellent instructions sealed into each bright yellow package.

Basic first aid techniques
Bleeding

Speed is of the essence when dealing with deep wounds. If you can't find a gauze pad or cloth quickly, apply pressure with your fingers. Keep pressure there until blood flow slows, even if you have to wind bandages around it. After that, clean the wound and dress it with a sterile gauze pad or sticking plaster.

Broken bones

The main aim in treating broken or fractured bones is to minimize further damage by keeping them still. For limbs, this means an improvized splint, such as a branch or a bike pump. A broken leg can be kept steady by binding it to the good one, with clothing used as padding in between. Fingers can also be tied to each other for support. Suspected spinal or neck injury usually means not moving the victim at all until suitable help arrives.

Emergency repairs:
The bike

Wilderness repairs by necessity have to be bodges. Their aim should be to get you home. Even the best equipped tourer doesn't carry a vice, a tool stand or an oxy-acetylene torch. And anyway, sod's law dictates that if you travel prepared for *almost* every eventuality, the part that breaks will be the single part you didn't bring.

Bodging with raw materials

Discarded bits of wire, stray pieces of wood, twigs and grass can all be used to bodge a variety of repairs. Zip-ties are also excellent for fixing all sorts of different problems – from a derailleur which is about to pop its clogs to mending a strut on a snapped pannier rack.

Puncture

Ready-glued patches weigh next to nothing and take up very little room. But, if the worst comes to the worst and you have a puncture when you don't have any patches left – and have used or lost your spare tube – you can ride quite successfully with a knotted tube. You tie the knot in the tube so that the hole is isolated.

Broken chain and broken chain tool

A thin piece of wire can hold the chain together at a pinch, as could a small twig bound in tape to keep it in position. You'll have to stay in the big ring so the wire doesn't catch on the other rings.

Tacoed wheel

With big fat tyres, tightly tensioned spokes and a conservative riding style it's tough to trash a wheel. But accidents, ahem, do happen and a taco-shaped wheel has to be straightened before you can even attempt to true it with a spoke tool (see page 122).

Push the wheel back into shape with all your weight (use feet if need be), or hit one of the four points of the shape hard on the ground.

Twisted rear mech

Should a stray branch wrap itself into the rear derailleur you've got problems if you don't brake straight away. Generally you spot the problem before it goes terminal but if not, you've got a bent hanger and a twisted derailleur. If the damage is bad you'll have to run the bike as a one-speed, bypassing the mech by placing the chain on one of the sprockets. You will need to shorten the chain with your chain tool for it to run smoothly.

Bent chainrings

Bent chainrings can be straightened with a small adjustable spanner and the application of a modicum of direct force. Be careful not to damage any of the teeth on the chain ring as these are not so easy to repair.

Trail-side repair skills can be learnt 'on the spot' but there's no substitute for experience. Learn how your machine works before heading for the wilds.

TIP

> Day riders who find themselves without repair patches or a spare tube have been known to stuff grass, straw, paper, or leaves in their tyre to at least get them home. The looks they must get though...

TOURING

Day rides – in nice weather, on a good bike, with the wind behind you – are great fun. They keep you fit and get you out into the fresh air. But, like all good things, they have to come to an end. At dusk you must go home.

By going long-distance cycle touring you can extend the enjoyment of a single day's cycling to a week, a fortnight, a month, or whatever takes your fancy.

Bicycles are load-carrying platforms – add to your frame some pannier racks and you have a machine that can take you away from it all for weeks on end. Load up a tent, a sleeping bag and a toothbrush and you have the perfect home on wheels.

To a couch-potato, a holiday which involves physical effort is a waste of energy. For bike tourers the expenditure of effort is part of the whole experience – it's gratifying to know you can pig out on multiple cream cakes and not pile on podge. Yet raising a sweat is only a small part of cycle touring, a means to an end. And the 'end' is to expand your horizons, not just geographically, but mentally as well. Travel broadens the mind by introducing you to new people and ways of life. Bicycles can transport you respectable distances without intimidating speed.

The main *raison d'etre* of cycle touring is freedom. The freedom to go where you like, at speeds which keep you in touch with your surroundings. An environmentally sensitive way to see the world. Travelling by cycle allows for genuine exploration away from the beaten paths which so often crawl with cars, coaches, lorries and other man-made contraptions out of step with the region you came to discover.

Slow but not too slow, cycling is the ideal way to see the world, either alone or with companions.

Bike tourists intrigue local people rather than confront them. Two-wheeled travellers will be stopped and offered fruit, free board-and-lodgings and help with navigation in some areas. Get your map out in a village and you'll be surrounded within minutes. A bicycle, with bags behind, is a mobile introduction agency. It's good to be exotic.

Requirements

Getting out into the back of beyond is not hard. It does not have to cost a lot of money. There are no age or sex barriers. Special equipment is useful but not absolutely necessary.

The biggest challenge for any potential adventurer is inertia, the desire to stay comfortable, not to rock the boat. Break free from such constraints and a self-propelled adventure becomes easy, whether it's a day out in neighbouring hills or an epic crossing of Australia.

> **TIP**
>
> **> A word of caution**: cycle touring is addictive. Once you've started you won't want to stop and all your holidays start to involve two wheels and a set of battered pannier bags. You have been warned!

But not everybody wants to cross continents. For many, three days in a national park would be adventure enough. Whilst not high adventure in the classic sense, small-scale expeditions are nevertheless fun for their own sake and may easily become trial runs for foreign jaunts. But if they are the sum of your ambitions, that's fine.

There is no rule that says a bike expedition has to be in foreign climes to qualify as 'adventurous'. Nor do you have to be young, fit and single. The requirement is not youth in itself, but a youthful outlook on life and a desire for new learning.

Types of tours

There are three levels of adventure which can be acheived through cycle touring: low adventure, medium adventure and high adventure.

These three levels often mark progressions to an ultimate goal. For some people, the ultimate goal is a very long time away from home, an exotic country, little cash, few clothes and a great deal of optimism. To start out at this third stage without the benefit of living through the first two would be exciting but foolhardy. Experience of cycling touring should be picked up gradually with day rides and weekend trips. Few people are ready to take on a major expedition without a great deal of preparation and practice. Organized tours are great for gaining vital experience.

Not everybody wants to progress to high adventure, and not everybody would consider low adventure to be tame. A non-outdoorsy person who had never slept in a tent before might consider a wet weekend at a sheltered camp-site as rather too much high adventure. To progress from such heights would be seen as next to impossible. It's not: it's just putting in the miles and gaining the experience.

LUGGAGE

As well as a strong, trusty bike you'll need bags to carry all your gear in. For short tours without camping equipment you could get away with front panniers and a 'rack-pack' (small bag which fixes on to the top of your rear rack). For tours involving camping gear you'll need front and rear panniers on special strong aluminium racks.

Rucksacks

Rucksacks are fine for short day rides or commuting but for more than an hour of riding a heavy rucksack is both inefficient and uncomfortable. Bumbags suffer from the same problems. Put the weight on the bike.

However, there are some good cycle rucksacks available which are ideal for commuting or rough mountain bike rides where pannier bags would rattle off. These rucksacks have pouches for helmets, pumps and other items.

Some pannier bags convert into rucksacks. They have integral shoulder straps hidden behind zipped panels. Alternatively, stash a bum-bag in a pannier and use it when extra capacity is needed away from the bike.

It's surprising how much luggage you can carry on a bike but be careful, an overloaded bike can become unwieldy.

Key features – pannier bags

> **Size, capacity and weight** – no need for huge panniers, 25 litres a piece for the rear and 10–15 for the front is more than adequate. Avoid the panniers with an integral rack-top section linking the two rear panniers – they tend to be cheap and nasty and are a poor use of rack space.

> **Quality of construction and durability of material** – many quality bags are made from Cordura nylon material. This is light, tough and very abrasion resistant. Traditional materials include 'cotton duck' which is bombproof but heavy.

> **Design features** – look for good fixing hooks, plenty of compartment spacers and pockets, reflective tape for safety, an overlapping lid to keep out rain, a stiff back so the pannier bags don't wobble into wheels, compression straps, carrying handles and reinforced key wear areas, such as where panniers attach to the rack.

Left: Rucksacks are ideal for short trips and rough terrain.

Above: A good seatpack can carry a windproof jacket.

TIPS

> Use zip-ties to make doubly sure pannier bags stay attached to racks. The ones that have a little catch so you can release them are very handy and can strap anything to anything. Carry at least twenty with you each trip. They weigh next to nothing.

> Most panniers will not be completely waterproof, so if in doubt wrap your kit in plastic bags for extra protection.

> **Weather proofing** – some panniers have integral covers, others are good enough to cope with a few hours of heavy rain but will leak eventually, especially when exposed to road splashing. Waterproof panniers such as Karrimor and Ortleib use welded seams instead of sewn ones, as well as waterproof fabric, to make panniers that can be completely immersed yet stay dry inside.

> **Mounting system** – look for spring-latch systems. These use plastic springs in the top hanging hooks which clamp to the pannier rack. These 'klick-fix' hooks are not very tough and can snap, so carry spares if you are going on an extended trip.

It's wise to carry spare pannier fixing hooks on longer rides. You should also make regular checks on the attaching screws to ensure they remain tight.

TOURING BIKES
AND HOW TO PACK THEM

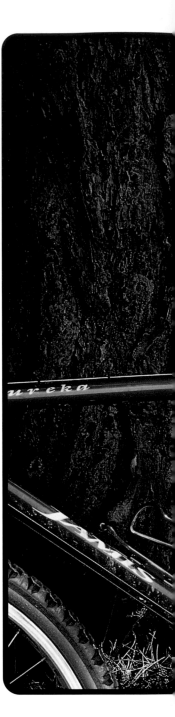

A touring bike or a hybrid bike (a mix between a touring bike and a mountain bike) is ideal for a road based tour. For long stretches of dirt tracks a mountain bike is more suitable, the stronger the better.

Whichever bike you choose make sure of the following: the bike has 'eyes' near the drop-outs for fixing pannier racks; it is comfortable for long distance riding with a well-padded saddle and cushioned handlebar tape or grips; and it's easy to maintain, so avoid unnecessarily complex moving parts such as fancy suspension forks (choose elastomer instead of oil-filled).

Pre-tour checks

Take your bike on a number of hard touring weekends before you embark on any epics. All the components and in particular the transmission system, ie the derailleur gears, the chain and chain-wheels should be bedded in and secure. Do not test anything on a tour. Every item should be familiar and 100% reliable.

Do as many trial runs as possible with your full touring kit before setting off. Don't load up the night before and then realize the amount of stuff you're carrying is warping your aluminium rack. There should be no surprises.

> **TIP**
>
> > If you're going for an extended trip abroad a steel frame is best. Back-street welders all over the world can fix steel but they can't weld titanium, carbon fibre or aluminium frames.

Packing it in

Weight

A bicycle is a load-carrying platform. It carries you, of course, but with pannier racks fitted it can also comfortably carry a great deal of luggage. Quite apart from actual weight, the way it's distributed in the pannier bags is important. Put the heaviest gear – tent, tool kit and cooking gear – at the bottom, close to the hubs.

Balance the load by making sure the pannier bags are of equal weight on each side. This should soon become a habit but initially, compare the weight by lifting one bag in each hand, using your arms as make-shift scales.

Rear panniers

This is where most of the weight goes. Pack heavy items low in the bags. Lots of compartments and external pockets will help you organize your kit. Use small nylon bags too.

Front panniers

Keep your front bags for light gear such as clothing. 'Low rider' front panniers, which are positioned on special racks directly over the front hub, offer greater stability than standard sling-over-the-front wheel bags.

Rackspace

Attach bulky items such as sleeping mats and tent poles to the rear rack using nylon straps. For extra luggage capacity use a rackpack, a bag specially designed to fit on the rear rack. These are often expandable and some convert

into rucksacks, making them ideal for taking off the bike when wandering around town.

Handlebar bags
Good for small items which need to be kept handy such as wallet, sunscreen, energy bars and fruit.

Carrying cameras
To prevent undue vibrations, pack camera equipment in the rear bag or in a padded rack-pack. Over the front wheel is not the best place because the vibration can shake even the toughest camera to pieces.

Bottle bags
If you carry drinking water on your back with a CamelBak you will have spare bottle cage capacity. Fit bottle bags, produced by Scott and other companies, and pack out with useful items such as, puncture repair patches, keys and spare energy bars.

Packing the bike
Try not to overload – 25lb (11kg) of kit in 70–80 litres (three cubic feet or so) of pannier bag space is more than enough for most trips of a week or over. Don't overload the front wheel – 8lb (3.5kg) is the maximum.

Don't forget to leave space for food, water and presents for the folks back home.

Main picture: Rear panniers can carry a lot. Pack heavy items low down.

Above: Where there's space there's room for a bag.

ULTRA LIGHTWEIGHT TOURING

Audax riders take to the mountains on the highest road in the French Pyrenees.

For those tourers who like the added spice of a fixed challenge on their holidays there are a number of organizations which 'award' points for miles covered or hills climbed. There are also clubs which promote group tours and rides over famous passes or along routes used by classic road races such as Paris-Roubaix and Milan-San Remo.

All these rides are non-competitive and are much like the charity rides in the UK such as the London-to-Brighton or the Great North Ride. You are free to choose your own time and speed but have to follow a set course, although there are often options such as longer or shorter sections. Even though they are not races it is better to use a road racing bike rather than a touring bike, although many participants do use their touring machines, pannier bags included.

Audax

This is an international association which promotes long distance group rides, usually at distances of 200, 300, 400 and 600 kilometres (125, 187, 250, 375 miles). These rides are non-competitive and have to be completed at an average speed of between 15 and 30km/h (10–20 mph approx). The best known Audax ride is the 1,200-kilometre (750-mile) Paris-Brest-Paris, which attracts up to 3,000 riders and is held every four years.

Audax UK is the UK representative of the Randonneurs Mondiaux international cycling movement. Many hundreds of riders of all ages qualify as 'randonneurs' each year by riding a 200km randonnee, or long distance ride. It's possible to go on to attain a 'super randonneur' award by completing a 200, 300, 400 and 600km (125–375 mile) series of rides.

In the UK, annual rides such as the 'Dorset Coast' attract hundreds of riders. For information contact Audax UK, 1 Bird Mews, Workingham, Berkshire RG40 1DZ.

TIP

> On most organized long-distance tours return transport is not provided so you should acquaint yourself with local train timetables or make sure there's a car waiting for you at the end.

Col bashers

The Ordre des Cols Durs (literally the 'Order of the Hard Cols') is a French touring club with branches all over the world, including Britain. The club promotes 'the active enjoyment of mountain regions by giving information and encouragement to pass-riding cyclists.' Members amass metres climbed per year. An average two week holiday in the Alps will tot up maybe 20,000 metres (65,000 feet) of climbing. British 'cols' are eligible but it's only in France where the naming, measuring, sign-posting and publicizing of mountain passes is taken so seriously. It's absolutely *de rigeur* to be photographed next to the signpost informing you of the col's name and how high above sea level you've climbed. For information contact OCD, 20 Spencer Gate, St. Albans, Hertfordshire AL1 4AD.

Classic road race tours

Paris-Roubaix, France

Run in mid-May over a 265km (165-mile) course, 57 km (35 miles) of it cobbled, the Paris-Roubaix tour is not for the faint-hearted. Some 1,500 or so riders pay 50 French francs to complete one of the toughest races in Europe. The tour starts in Compiegne, 75km (47 miles) north of Paris. For those who wish to spread the ride over two days the 'Tourist Formula' allows a night in Solesmes after 118km (74 miles). For further information you can contact Velo Club de Roubaix, 73 Avenue du Parc des Sports, F-591000, Roubaix.

Milan-San Remo, Italy

This is the classic Italian race, run in mid-September over a reasonably flat course of 290km (180 miles). The weather and scenery are the two main attractions of this event and at least 1,500 riders take part each year. The ride is open to clubs only and individuals have to have a letter from their club confirming the member has adequate third party insurance. For more information contact Unione Cicloturistica San Remo, c/o Bar Ciclosport, Corso Inglesi 294, 1-18038 San Remo, Italy.

Europa Cup Marathons

These are exceptionally tough organized tours that take place in the mountains of Austria, Germany and Italy. They were started in 1987 in order to test the endurance capacity of the fittest cycle tourists. There are six events per year and each participant receives an individually numbered racing jersey. Riders who successfully complete at least three of the six annual tours also receive awards and certificates. Each year only 500 entrants are allowed to compete and pressure for places is always fierce.

For further information about these events contact VCR-Regensburg, EC-Organisation-Komitee, Pflanzen-mayer strasse 8a, 8400 Regensburg, Germany.

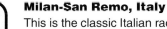

Above: Essentials only – pump, spare tube and energy food.

Right: Audax may be non-competitive, but you still receive medals for your stamina-sapping achievements.

TOURING WITHOUT A TENT

Bike exploration without equipment such as tents, sleeping bags and other heavy items is often referred to as credit-card touring because it's the ultimate in lightweight adventure

Credit-card touring has a lot going for it: you don't have to carry too much kit so your bike isn't laden down and you also get to stay in different buildings every night, some posh, others basic, but all, hopefully, will provide you with the use of a bath or a shower.

After a hard day's riding in the rain it's the height of luxury to turn up at a hotel or B&B. Check in advance whether mud will be a problem and also check that there's a safe place to leave your bike.

Hotels and B&Bs

If your idea of staying the night somewhere doesn't involve sharing the bedroom with 20 others, a hotel or B&B is your best option. They are not cheap of course, so you need a large budget if you want to turn up at whatever hotel you find at the end of the day. Compared to campsites, especially wild ones, amenities will be first class and there's the added attraction of a substantial cooked breakfast. If you're travelling in the holiday season you may need to book ahead.

Youth Hostels

Despite their title, youth hostels are open to members of any age and many now offer family rooms as well as dormitory accommodation. Hostels, whether run by one of the national associations or as independent ventures, range from smart city centre hotels to simple, candle-lit stone buildings in the middle of nowhere. A major part of their appeal is the individual character they build up through location, layout and the personality of the wardens. Within the national associations, there has been a trend towards upgrading facilities as the notion of running them as businesses has taken hold. On the whole, these facilities are excellent but prices have risen accordingly. Many diehards still resent the fact that hostellers are as welcome if they travel by car as on foot or cycle. This trend, however, has allowed private hostels to flourish, especially in remote areas.

SUPPORTED TOURS

The Cyclists' Touring Club and many specialist companies run organized tours. The
organizers are selling experience: they have
done it all many times before and know the
score. Your route is planned and your accommodation booked in advance, so rather than
get bogged down in bureaucracy, you can con-
centrate on the cycling. On some supported
tours a 'sag-wagon' will be close behind,
lugging all your gear. If your lack of fitness gets the better of you, it's simple to
hop on the back of the truck and hitch a ride
until you've recovered.

TIP

> Before checking in for
the evening in a hotel or
B&B, make sure there's
somewhere secure for the
bike. What the reception
staff think is 'secure' may
be very different to your
definition. A lock-up
garage is ideal; round the
back by the bins is not.

Camping Barns and Bunkhouses

Camping barns and bunkhouses are popular in some English National
Parks and are especially widespread in the Derbyshire Peak District, which
set up a network in the early 1980s. You don't need to be a member to stay
in camping barns, but you do need to book in advance.

Often referred to as stone tents, camping barns offer very basic facilities with solid permanent protection from the weather being the key factor
in design. Usually single storey, most have a sleeping area, sometimes a
raised platform like alpine huts, and another part set aside for cooking and
eating. Similar in price to an overnight stay at a campsite, they cut out the
necessity of carrying your own tent and finding a suitable site. However,
you do need to bring your own sleeping bag, cooking gear and food. Toilet
facilities and drinking water are usually available but heating is not.

Bunkhouses offer a wider range of facilities, usually of a higher standard than camping barns. Dormitory sleeping arrangements are usually
split into male and female rooms, with sometimes the option of rooms for
two or three people. Bunk beds with mattresses are standard and most
have a common room for relaxation as well as a fully equipped kitchen, a
drying room, showers, flush toilets and central heating. Inevitably, they are
more expensive than camping barns and prices vary considerably
between the wide variety of independents as well as those established by
National Parks and other authorities.

**Whether you are staying in a tent or a hotel
always ensure that your belongings are safe
and secure!**

Bothies

Scottish camping barns are called bothies.
These used to be lonely stone buildings out in
the sticks, offering only the most spartan of
comforts, usually just a roof and four walls.
Nowadays many have been spruced up and significantly upgraded. Those in very remote areas
continue to offer only very basic amenities and
because of their remoteness are free to stay in
overnight. The truly remote ones should not be
thought of as a base for a camping holiday but
as emergency accommodation only.

TOURING WITH A TENT

Carrying your own home on the bike gives you options. There's no rush to reach town by the end of the day and you can choose to set up camp at a particularly scenic spot. With camping gear on board you can also hunker down in the middle of the day if it starts raining heavily or a sand storm blows up.

The Nylon Option:
Tents and Sleeping Bags
There's nothing quite like transforming a patch of open countryside into a cozy haven against the worst excesses of weather while still feeling completely in tune with the elements. Lying snug and warm in your sleeping bag, protected by the shelter you have erected is a particularly enjoyable experience.

Tents:
From Ridge to Geodesic
Tents are designed to offer you easily portable, lightweight protection, not just from the elements but also from curious eyes and nasty insects. Modern tents, especially the lightweight, backpacking ones, usually create this protection with a double-wall design – the tent has a 'breathable' inner with a sewn-in groundsheet and a waterproof outer (fly).

The range of quality lightweight tents available offers extensive variations in design, weight, materials and function. Whatever your plans, you'll almost certainly want a tent to suit a variety of conditions so compromises will have to be made to balance durability, price, size and weight.

Tent design has received a lot of attention in recent years and there are many different basic designs, hybrids and extensions to choose from ranging from traditional 'ridge' and bungalow-like frames to elongated geodesic domes – almost works of art!

Materials
Most lightweight tent fly sheets are made from coated nylon or polyester fabric, with the prime aim of being totally waterproof. Seams, zips, pegging points and guylines are all potential weaknesses and subject to great tensions.

Some tents have an inner which is all mesh – this keeps the mosquitoes out but allows an unimpeded view of the night sky. You need to be confident that it won't rain before going to sleep without the flysheet over the inner!

Stoves and cooking
A lightweight stove is a brilliant investment, giving warm food and hot tea in all weather; the hard part is choosing from the wide range of styles and fuel capabilities. There are no absolutes in fuel choice. Gas, petrol, meths, paraffin, special fuels – they all have their pros and cons.

Gas
Pro – clean burning, simple burners, relatively low carbon monoxide production, good cartridge availability in Europe.
Con – weight of cartridges, price.

Lightweight hoop tents pack away small and are surprisingly roomy. They are also quick to erect.

Petrol

Pro – easy availability, good heat output.
Con – high carbon monoxide output, volatile, can be awkward to operate, motor fuel additives induce 'coking' in the burner. White gas, such as Coleman fuel, doesn't have the additives present in both leaded and unleaded petrol and is far better when available.

Paraffin

Pro – available worldwide except the US, cheap, good heat, not as volatile as petrol.
Con – rather smelly, can be difficult to light, stoves need regular cleaning.

Meths

Pro – easy to light, unpressurized burners, not volatile.
Con – availability, performance/weight ratio and control are not very good; difficult to light below 0°C (32°F).

Above: You soon find out whether you get on with your travelling companion. Small tents offer no escape.

TIP

> Only use your stove inside the tent if the weather leaves you no option. Take great care to keep flapping nylon away from the flame and ventilate well as it's easy to get carbon monoxide poisoning.

Sleeping Bags

Whatever the design or filling used, all sleeping bags work by trapping warm, still air to provide a layer of insulation.

Down filling: Down, plucked from water fowl, is an excellent insulator. It weighs far less and compresses into a far smaller volume than any synthetic fill to achieve the same warmth factor.

Man-made fillings: Synthetic fibres are cheaper, absorb little water and retain their warmth value when damp. Rapid advances in the last decade mean synthetic wadding is fast approaching the warmth and low bulk ratio of down.

Warmth variables and cost: The usual method of rating a sleeping bag's warmth – not perfect because everyone has their own warmth requirements – is the 'seasons' rating.

1 season – typical UK summer nights
2 season – late spring through to early autumn
3 season – for use in all but winter conditions
4 season – all year use, including cold conditions

TOURING CHECKLIST

This is a list of touring items taken on a typical lightweight expedition abroad. It can be reduced for mild-weather UK and credit-card tours but there's not that much difference between the requirements for a fortnight's road-touring in Yorkshire and a month-long solo mountain bike expedition to Iceland.

No published list can meet your exact needs so if you need to pack your teddy bear or an electric shaver, that's up to you. Use this list as a memory jogger, mixing and matching to suit your own requirements and the demands of your tour.

Choose gear that is light and compact but don't sacrifice quality. Comfort costs.

Food and cooking
>Stove
>Fuel bottle
>Stove repair kit
>Waterproof/windproof matches (emergency only), matches and/or lighter
>Lightweight cooking pots
>Coleman's mug or plastic cup
>Spoon
>Swiss Army knife
>Dehydrated food (emergency only)
>Food staples: oats, tea bags, sugar, pasta, quick-cook rice, herbs and spices
>Energy bars
>Salt
>Flexible water carriers or jerry cans
>Water purifying apparatus
>Iodine tincture or
>Puritabs

Camping
>Mosquito net
>Tent
>Sleeping mattress
>Sleeping bag
>Toilet paper
>Torch (or front cycle light)
>Rear LED
>Spare batteries
>Candle

Medical
>First aid kit including antiseptic cream.
>MASTA syringe kit
(for travel to tropical countries)

Clothing
>Two T-shirts
>Thin fleece or PowerStretch top
>Two wickable base layers
>Waterproof shell layer
>Ultra-lightweight Pertex windproof
>Thermal tights
>Two pairs of cycle shorts
>Three pairs of socks
>One set of underwear
>One shirt
>One pair of light gloves
>One pair of water-

Make your own written checklist. That way you should avoid missing small easily forgotten items like lipsalve (above) compasses (left) and the rest.

proof over-gloves
>Silk headover
>Fleece hat
>Baseball cap
>Helmet
>Sunglasses
>Spectacles or contact lenses (plus prescription in case of breakages)
>Cycling shoes
>Flip-flops or similar
>Cycling mitts

Hygiene
>Detergent
>Soap
>Toothbrush
>Comb
>Small bottle of shampoo
>Sewing kit
>Suncream
>Lip salve

Maintenance
>20 reusable zip-ties
>Bike tools (see list on page 106)

Essential Equipment
>Camera and film
>Passport
>Pens and a pencil
>Money, travellers cheques and credit card
>Six passport booth photos
>Airline, train or boat tickets
>Numbers card (numbers of travellers cheques, passport etc.)
>Watch
>Maps
>Compass

It would be mighty tough to forget a tent or sleeping bag, but a mug and the coffee to go in it can easily be left behind. The best way to make sure you pack everything you need is to collect items over a few days – perhaps in a special box. A last minute dash is a recipe for omissions.

EXPEDITIONS

An expedition is a journey into the unknown, a chance to dabble with freedom. Whether it's with ten fellow cyclists, one partner or just solo, an expedition is an adventure.

But an expedition doesn't have to mean trans-Sahara jaunts or cross-Himalaya epics. Just as much adventure can be had much closer to home and on a tight budget. Families can have expeditions. Lone grandmothers can have expeditions. It's a cliché, but the most basic rule in cycle travel is that there are no rules.

When touring in the back of beyond – this is the Sonora desert in Mexico – you have to carry everything you'll need including your accomodation.

A wet but happy cyclist caught in a Zambian rain storm.

EQUIP THYSELF

Spending a fortune on the best bike and state-of-the-art expedition equipment is no guarantee of a problem-free trip. It's attitude that counts, not how good your gear is. But it can't be escaped that there is a certain minimum outlay.

Expedition fitness

Because a bicycle is a supportive platform it isn't all that tiring to do some quite respectable distances. A novice walker attempting to do a 20-mile hike needs to be pretty fit. A beginner doing the equivalent on a bike need only be marginally fit. Walkers have to propel themselves by their own efforts at all times. A cyclist can get 'free rides' by coasting and going downhill. All of this means a cyclist can travel meaningful distances without being super-fit. Continuous and relevant exercise, such as cycling for a number of days, quickly leads to fitness.

So long as you take the first few days gently, fitness will come easily and progressively. Of course, the fitter you are before you go – the higher the level of fitness you'll attain once out in the back of beyond.

TIP

> A reasonably fit cyclist can easily manage 70 miles (112km) a day on flat tarmac roads. Fit tourers can pedal up to 120 miles (193km) a day, especially in the summer when daylight lasts longer. Mountain bikers on dirt roads can manage 50-60 miles (80-96km) a day depending on the roughness of the track. However, the rule of thumb should be to minimize the distance to maximize the enjoyment. Take your time, it's not a race!

The Expedition Machine

A reliable bike of lasting value does not come cheap. For touring it's possible to travel with a budget bike (£300 and below) but as touring puts a lot of stress on components it's better to invest in a stronger, more reliable groupset.

For rough ctuff touring it would be sensible to choose a mountain bike, but a beefed-up 'touring bike' from manufacturers such as Dawes and Raleigh can in fact tackle a surprisingly wide range of terrain, from tarmac to corrugated tracks.

Starting out

Your first expedition is not going to be a bed of roses. Expect pain. Expect to jettison half of your gear. Expect mistakes. But don't be put off. Your first major tour needn't be your last.

The most important step – after the germ of the idea has taken control of your whole system – is actually to get out there and do it. Too many people have great ideas for trips but never actually get round to doing them. Don't be one of these people. Promise yourself you'll do the trip. If not now, set a date sometime soon. After the first simple tour – a weekend break somewhere close to home is a fine start – you'll progress to bigger and better things.

Fancy a year cruising the world on a bike, or even just a month spinning through the Algarve? Stop dreaming, do it. Got a job? Leave it. Too many commitments? Dump them. Think you're too old/fat/shy/poor? You're not. Stop making excuses.

Don't let life pass you by. Plan your first expedition now. You won't regret it.

Whatever the style of bike, spending more gets you:

> **strength:** a more expensive bike is generally stronger than a cheap one despite being lighter.

> **more precise gear shifting, braking and handling:** this is where the extra expense starts to be worth it. On a long tour or tough back-country trip with no bike shops nearby, you need gears and brakes which will not let you down.

> **exotica:** front suspension forks can make a massive improvement in rider comfort on an expedition. Good quality ones offer the best comfort in the widest range of conditions.

BICYCLE RACING

At the turn of the century, bicycles were the fastest things on the road, and many young men took delight in scorching past horse-drawn carriages. Nowadays bikes may seem slow. Modern transport has desensitized us to speed, and from a car window 40 mph is unremarkable.

But if you're riding a bike it's a different story. When you're pelting downhill with the wind rushing past your ears and the tarmac whipping away beneath you, 40mph is very fast indeed. On a bicycle you rediscover speed.

Why race?

That's one reason why racing bikes is so much fun: it's a big adrenaline buzz, whether you're racing round a town centre criterium circuit, or leaping rocks in a dry stream bed on your MTB.

As in any sport, there's the competition angle, the striving to win. But there's a lot more to cycle racing than, say, athletics, where the fastest man or woman always wins. You have to use your head too.

You're going fast enough for aerodynamics to matter, which makes race tactics and riding technique crucial, and you're controlling a bit of machinery as well as your own legs, so skill plays a greater role too.

You can do it

Bicycle racing is a great leveller. If you can ride a bike, you can have a crack at it. You don't have to be a muscular sports jock to compete. Bantamweights can take on heavyweights and win. It's your power-to-weight ratio that matters.

Cycling is very forgiving if you're starting off overweight too, since the bike bears the weight of your body. Easy? No, but painless compared to jogging or squash.

At its other extreme, cycling is *the* sport if you want to test and extend the limits of your physical fitness. Cyclists can and do reach levels of exhaustion impossible in other sports, because the bike allows you to push yourself beyond the point of collapse. Consequently professional cyclists are among the fittest athletes in the world.

Getting started

All you need to get started is a bike, a helmet (usually), and either a race licence or a small entry fee. Events are often listed in cycling magazines or displayed in bike shops. If you're a member of a cycling organization – which is mandatory for some races – you'll be sent race details in the post.

Races exist for all levels of ability, from young children, through novice adults, right up to professionals. Your level of involvement in racing depends on your attitude and ambition. Many mountain bikers turn up at the odd weekend race for a bit of fun, rather than with any intention of winning. Some road racers make cycling their religion, ritually shaving their legs, monitoring their diet and doing 30-mile training rides after work.

The best advice is to avoid the blinkered attitude which some cyclists bring to their sport, and have a go at each event as and when you can. Go for it – and have fun.

Left: A road bike is just about the fastest way to travel using your own power, and you really feel the speed.

Below: Downhill mountain biking is like downhill skiing – fast, thrilling, and with plenty of opportunities for spectacular crashes. Full face helmets and body armour are vital.

MTB DOWNHILL RACING

Top level downhill mountain biking is a spectator sport that lasts for no more than five or six minutes, can be decided on tenths of a second and is populated by what can most diplomatically be described as 'characters'.

It's a sport that combines the bulked-out outfits of ice-hockey and the technological wizardry of Formula One with the speed and panache of skiing.

But unlike skiing this is a sport that is as much at home in the grassy Yorkshire Dales as in the snowy Swiss Alps. With a £400 bike (don't spend less) you too can downhill. There's nothing quite like a 40mph fire-road descent for quickening the pulse.

If you don't like crashing, don't become a downhiller; eating dirt is all too common.

Crazy

A top-class downhiller may appear crazed and out of control but underneath that Darth Vader mask sits a brain that is acutely aware of what will happen if the adrenaline rush clouds the judgment. The best downhillers are cool and calculating, fully aware of how to control their bikes at all times. What may look like an undignified slide may, in fact, be an inch-perfect drift.

Technique

Novice downhill riders should expect to have a few monumental crashes to begin with – it really is an important part of the fun – but choose your practice slopes carefully, go for grass rather than rocks.

To progress you have to be at one with the bike. Keep fluid, let the bike do the talking and don't tense up, otherwise all you will do is upgrade your nervous wobble into a faceplant.

Don't think about that ditch in front of you; you should be focussing on the next corner. Clearing the ditch should become instinctive through practice.

Racing

There are currently no restrictions on who can race on downhill courses so if you've got a bike and a helmet you're equipped to enter a race. For notification of future events look at the race posters in your local bike shop or check listings in the specialist press.

Race fitness

And don't think that downhill is the easy option in mountain biking. Just because you've got gravity on your side doesn't mean you don't have to pedal. If you want to go fast down hill you've still got to work hard.

Once you've mastered the art of smooth, fluid descending it's time to enter races. There's

TIP

> Body armour, despite its appearance, will not enable you to survive a 50mph crash into a tree. Don't let protective clothing fool you into thinking you can go faster. Armour may prevent abrasion injuries but won't prevent broken bones or worse if you hit something solid at speed.

bound to be some near where you live. There's always a hill somewhere. Even when it's just a pimple, course organizers will make it seem like you're shooting the Eiger by adding dirt ramps, sharp corners and sudden deviations.

Competitive downhilling is all about racing against the clock. But you can have just as much fun downhilling without the pressures of time. Adventure travel companies organize mountain bike touring holidays to countries all around the world (most notably Morocco) where every day is spent downhilling. A four-wheel drive carts you to a new summit each day.

Ski resort areas have also cottoned on to the sheer thrill of downhilling and in the summer open up their ski lifts to descent freaks so they can take the plunge without the sweat.

Protection

A good helmet is vital. Spend at least £30. If you want to get serious take a look at full-face helmets (£70–120).
The professionals use body armour (£60–150).
Always wear gloves: gravel palm slides hurt.

Bikes

For advice on front and rear suspension systems, exotic frame materials and twist-grip gear changers go to a quality bike shop. Entry level race machines start at about £1,200 and rise to £3,500+. Novices needn't spend anywhere near this much. A good basic £400 mountain bike will be strong enough for beginners. Add suspension forks later (£200–500).

MTB CROSS-COUNTRY RACING

In a little over a decade mountain bike racing has gone from being a minority sport invented by Californian hippies – where it was fine to stop half way round the course for a cigarette – to being a full-blown Olympic discipline with professional riders and big-budget teams.

The spirit of the early days lives on though and mountain bike racing can be as frenetic or as relaxed as you want it to be. You can aim to do well in your class or you can make a point of coming in last, deliberately stopping to admire the view and help stranded racers mend their punctures.

It really is the taking part that counts. Of course, at the top of each class of riders there are those who take the whole thing seriously but for the great majority of riders it's a day out riding with friends and fellow enthusiasts, a chance to see what everybody else is riding and to hang out at the finish area and cheer on the other classes.

Cost

Races cost £5–£10 to enter and on the surface you don't get a lot for this. No T-shirt, no drink and no medal for finishing. But a lot of work has gone on behind the scenes. Most races are on closed circuits – walkers and horse-riders are not allowed so your entry fee gets you a moan-free race-track – and this requires a lot of negotiation with land-owners. Attendance at the event by medics also costs money, as does the provision of porta-loos and a sound system.

Categories

Before you start racing you need to work out who you should be competing against. Categories are sorted by age, ability and sex.

Pee-wees	kids aged 3–6
Sprogs	kids aged 7–11
Youth	12–15
Junior	16–18
Senior	19–39
Vets	40–49
Masters	50+

Above these categories there are overall classes. These are 'fun' (for those who don't want to suffer); 'novice' (for newcomers); 'sport' (intermediate racers); 'experts' (serious racers) and 'pro/elite' (the creme de la creme).

Speed machine

There's no need to go out and buy a special race bike, so long as the mountain bike you currently own is well looked after and isn't a cheap and nasty one. Most bikes costing £250 and up will be fine for racing. You can always spend more when you improve your skills and need greater performance. Invest in front suspension as soon as you can afford it; it's worth an extra 10mph for downhill sections.

Race training

At its simplest level, training is just getting out on the bike regularly and testing yourself against friends. If you get serious you'll want to invest in a heart rate monitor, you'll join a gym and you'll spend a small fortune on carbohydrate energy bars!

What many would-be racers forget is that exercise recovery time is just as important as the hours spent on the bike. It's vital to rest so the body can catch up with the stresses you've been putting it under.

To improve as a racer you'll need to work on three key areas:
1. Endurance – putting in the miles, on a road bike as well as an MTB
2. Power – explosive sprints up short hill climbs
3. Speed – sprints and interval training.
Get specific advice from the trainers at your nearest sports centre.

Keep hydrated

It's critical to drink often during exercise, especially when racing. A water loss of just 5% can reduce muscular work capacity by 30%. When thirst hits you're already dehydrated. Many racers use CamelBaks – a plastic bladder in a slim rucksack. A tube and bite valve lets you suck out water. With this tube draped over your shoulder it's easy to stay hydrated.

When 'hanging out' at a weekend race (left) you spend a lot of time socialising... sometimes you even manage to ride round the course (main picture).

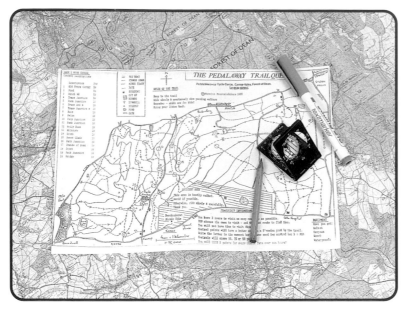

MTB ORIENTEERING

There are two basic types of MTB orienteering events:

1. Polaris Challenge

This is a two-day event for teams of two riders. The teams have a set number of checkpoints to reach and are given a special map. Some of the checkpoints are easy to locate but carry few points; other checkpoints carry maximum points but are far away and difficult to find. A fit team with little navigation experience may prefer to do high mileages to get to far-flung, easy-to-spot checkpoints whereas a slower team may opt to do less riding but more intensive map-work. The points accrued during the weekend determine the winning team.

Racers camp overnight and are totally self-sufficient. They have to carry camping and cooking kit on their bikes or in rucksacks. Polaris events tend to be run in wilderness areas and in challenging weather conditions.

2. Trailquest

These are single-day orienteering events which are much easier than Polaris events. They tend not to be as competitive and they are in less remote areas. They are, nevertheless, a great deal of fun and some Forest Enterprise woodlands have permanent Trailquest areas where you can buy a map and tick off the checkpoints.

Navigation

If you have a map and a compass and can spot two or more landmarks that can be identified on your map, you will easily find your approximate position by 're-section' (below).

Re-section

Select two landmarks that are spaced well apart. Take your compass in the palm of your hand and point the travel arrow at one of your chosen landmarks. Sight along the travel arrow by squinting and then slowly bring the compass down to chest level. Now twist the compass housing until the north needle and the northwards-pointing orientating arrow match. The bearing of this first landmark is the number that is situated above the index marker line. Memorize this number and then take the bearing for the other landmark.

These bearings are magnetic (compass) bearings. Because of the constantly changing nature of the Earth's magnetic field, magnetic bearings vary by a few degrees from true map (grid) bearings. To convert magnetic bearings to grid bearings, you have to remove this magnetic variation – it will be about 6.5 degrees. There is a mnemonic which should help you to

remember to remove the variation: MUGS – Magnetic Unto Grid Subtract.

To find your position in relation to these two identifiable features, take the first grid bearing you memorized and set it on to the compass dial. Put the compass on to the map. Place the direction line (the side edge of the compass base plate which is parallel to the travel arrow) over the first landmark and balance it on this point. Now swivel the compass until the orientating lines – inside the compass housing and pointing north – become parallel with the grid lines of the map. Where the edge of the compass lies now makes a line from the landmark to your approximate position.

MTB orienteering events are excellent opportunities to learn the kind of navigation techniques you need to explore wilderness areas safely.

TIP

> The beauty of orienteering events is that brains often beat brawn. A team with good navigation skills can beat a team of professional racers.

Selecting a route

Move from obvious small landmark to obvious small landmark. This means taking a bearing to an obvious feature; when you get there, you will know exactly where you are so you can start the process again.

Alternatively, you can make a deliberate error in following your bearing – aim off to one side of where you want to go and then when you reach a linear feature turn in the opposite direction to this original 'error'. Try always to use linear features such as rivers and field boundaries as a definite means of guidance.

To move from landmark to landmark, select your next destination and pinpoint your present one. With the compass edge, link the two up, using the travel arrow as the direction of travel at all times. Keep the compass flat and steady; then swivel the housing until the interior orientating lines become parallel to the map grid lines. Read off the bearing. Now you must convert this grid (map) bearing into a magnetic (compass) one. This time add the 6.5 degrees. (The mnemonic for this is GUMA: Grid Unto Magnetic Add.) Swivel yourself around until the north point of the needle aligns itself with the north point of the interior orientating arrow. To set off in the right direction, ensure the needles stay aligned and move in the direction that the travel arrow indicates.

Modern BMXs are much bettter than those of the 1980s due partly to the influence of mountain biking.

BMX AND OBSERVED TRIALS

Pulling wheelies on a bike is a basic urge. It's almost the first thing you do when you get on a mountain bike. Stunt riding is the natural extension of this urge, testing your skills over a set of obstacles. There are two forms of stunt riding: BMX, which predated mountain biking, and Observed Trials, which also predated mountain biking but is now fully absorbed within it.

BMX

Before mountain biking became popular in the late 1980s every kid aspired to a BMX bike. These were first and foremost fun bikes, perfect for stunts, tricks and short-course races. With the advent of mountain bikes, interest in BMXs waned, although a hard-core of riders still favoured them.

Today the scene is very different to the heady days of the mid-1980s. BMXs aren't kids bikes anymore, they are expensive, specialized machines generally bought and ridden by adults. BMX racing used to be very popular in the 1980s but the scene has withered, though not died out completely. If you want to go fast on a BMX-style bike it's probably best to use a mountain bike and enter standard MTB events. BMX nowadays means freestyle: riding half-pipes and performing tricks.

The trials events at race meetings always attract good crowds. Obstacles such as the log pile test the riders' skill, in particular their balance, to the limit.

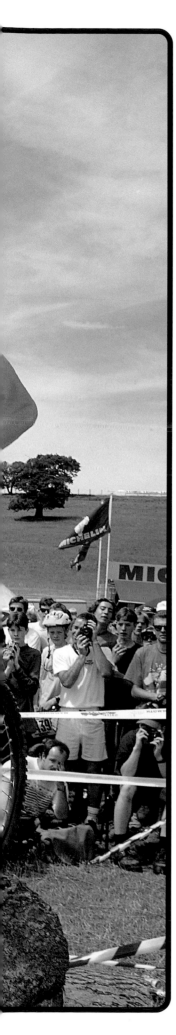

BMX Freestyle

There are three main disciplines within BMX freestyle. Riders tend to specialize in one of the three disciplines.

Street-riding is the most popular discipline because it requires no special venues, you just ride where the fancy takes you. Jumps are performed off mini-ramps but the trick most likely to upset bystanders is 'grinding', using the axle pegs on the wheel nuts to grind along hand-rails or park benches.

Flatland riding is performed on flat concrete and consists of choreographed, skilful tricks such as the various permutations of spinning the bike beneath the rider.

The most spectacular discipline is verting, getting 'big air' off ramps and half-pipes and pulling various spinning tricks at the same time. This is the kind of BMXing seen in demonstrations at public shows.

The bike

BMX bikes (the initials come from Bicycle Motocross) have small 20-inch wheels and diminutive chromoly frames. Being small, light and agile they can pull tricks no other bikes can manage. A good quality basic BMX will cost £200–300 with off-the-shelf pro bikes costing £500–800.

Accessories

BMX riders shun helmets but very often wear knee and elbow pads. Cycle mitts are a good idea for beginners because crashes, albeit at slow speeds, are guaranteed.

Observed Trials

This is where the rider has to negotiate obstacles and is awarded points for completing a course in a certain time and without touching feet on the ground. Spills are common but so

The ability to pull off impressive stunts guarantees you attention anywhere.

are skills and it's truly awe-inspiring to watch adept trials riders handling mountain bikes like they were welded to them.

A typical course is made up of ten or more linked sections with riders having to clear the course as best they can in three attempts. Five penalty points can be lost per section and this occurs if a rider dabs (touches) the ground, a tree, an obstacle (other than one that is meant to be hit) or a spectator. Zero points are awarded for a clean run, with 150 given against you for hitting everything in your path.

The Trials bike

An ordinary mountain bike and a skilled rider can do well in an observed trial but riders with special bikes have clear advantages. Built-for-the-purpose trials bikes have bash-plates fitted to protect the single chainwheel, are squatter than ordinary mountain bikes, have a single low gear and often have very fat tyres, bigger than the 2.1 inch tyres fitted to mountain bikes. They also have higher bottom brackets and steep frame angles.

Trials riders, like BMX riders, generally use conventional flat pedals with no retention devices and ride in soft shoes which help them 'feel' and grip the bike.

TIP

> To practise stunt riding you can set up your own 'soft' set of obstacles by using old car tyres. Line them up on top of each other to create pseudo-log jumps. Rubber won't damage chainrings. Once you've mastered the basic techniques use real obstacles but fit a chainring guard.

TIME TRIALLING

Time trialling is the simplest form of racing: one cyclist riding against the clock over a fixed distance, or trying to ride as far as possible in a fixed time. Time trials are commonly raced over 10, 25, 50 and 100 miles, and over 1, 12 and 24 hours. Riders set off at intervals and are forbidden to ride together at any time.

Aerodynamics is everything in time trialling. There's no one to shelter you from the wind, so you must slice through it like a knife. Bikes are streamlined to the limit, and so is the rider; pointy aero-helmets, tri bars, and Lycra skinsuits are the norm.

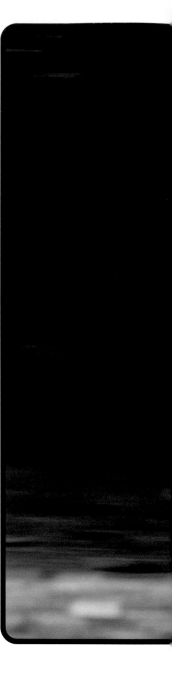

Time trial courses

Time trials are held on public roads, which in all but the biggest events are not usually closed to traffic. The course could be anywhere, in theory, but many are on dual carriageways and long flat main roads as these allow faster times to be achieved. They are the best way for riders aiming to improve their personal best (PB) times to assess their progress, so events such as these are always extremely popular.

In Europe time trials are typically run as part of a stage race; in Britain they are a popular sport in themselves, overseen by a governing body, the Road Time Trials Council. Time trials are run in the evenings and at weekends throughout the spring and summer. Each event is a race in its own right, but the aggregate results of three rides (a 50-mile, 100-mile and 12-hour TT) go towards the Best British All Rounder (BBAR) competition.

Time trials also make an appearance in the Olympics, both on road and track. The World Hour record is essentially a time trial held on the velodrome track.

Good for beginners

Time trialling is known as the race of truth for good reason: you can't make excuses; you've only got yourself to answer to. Time trialling can hurt, frankly. You're riding just the right side of oxygen debt for minutes or hours on end.

Despite this, time trialling is an excellent introduction to bicycle racing. For one thing, it doesn't matter how good you are. There is a winner, but you are only really racing against yourself, and won't get left off the back and demoralized like you might in a massed start race. Time trialling teaches you to ride hard and fast. If you go on to try massed start races, you'll know how far you can push yourself.

**Above left:
Tri bars enable the triallist to become as aerodynamic as possible.**

**Above right:
Britain's Chris Boardman is one of the world's greatest time triallists. Note how low his tuck is.**

Equipment for a time trial

You can ride a time trial on anything – even a mountain bike with slick tyres – but the more aerodynamic you get, the faster you'll be. Carbon fibre bikes with knife-like frame sections are ridden by Olympic contenders. Lesser mortals can just adapt a standard road bike.

First addition should be a set of clip-on tri bars (aerobars). These allow you to adopt the same arms-out-in-front position of the downhill skier, and reduce drag by anything up to 25%, depending on your current riding position.

Disk wheels and tri-spoke wheels are more aerodynamic than conventional spoked wheels, which churn the air like egg whisks. They are less safe in cross-winds, however. The front wheel is sometimes smaller (26 or 24 inches) to lower the front of the bike and make the rider more aerodynamic.

Gears are a 'straight-through block', meaning that the sprockets on the cassette will go up in steps of one tooth. This means the gears are closer together than on a road bike. Some riders time trial on a fixed gear.

A cycle computer will tell you how fast you're going, and most display average speed and trip distance too – very useful when there's no one to gauge your effort by. Pulse monitors are even better: they show your heart rate, so you can judge exactly how hard you are riding and how hard you should be riding.

ROAD RACING

High speeds and a huge field of riders split into teams make road racing one of the most tactical of cycle sports. In time trialling the man who rides fastest wins. In a road race it can be the man who rides smartest.

Stage races

Stage races are the biggest and most impressive of road races, and include the Tour de France, the Giro d'Italia, and the Tour DuPont. They last from five days to three weeks. Riders cycle distances of about 75–150 miles each day, day in, day out. Most stage races include a time trial, and some a team time trial or a criterium.

A stage race is won by the rider with the lowest cumulative time. This rider also wears the leader's jersey – the yellow jersey in the Tour de France – during the race. There are often jerseys for other riders too. In the Tour de France there's the green jersey for the best sprinter, and the polka-dot jersey for the King of the Mountains, the most consistent climber.

Stage races are gruelling events. The riders are in the saddle for up to six hours a day, riding at speeds of over 20 mph. To do this they need to consume 8,000–9,000 calories each day.

Above: The three Tour de France jerseys. Note how much bigger Indurain, the time trial specialist (in yellow) is than Virenque, the climber (in polka-dot).

The tactics

Most road race tactics hinge around drafting, which is when one rider cycles in the slipstream of another. By doing this the following rider can conserve up to 30% of his energy, and so 'rest' while on the move.

To draft effectively, you have to be close on the wheel of the leading rider – within about three feet (less than 1m), though the better rider you are the closer you can safely go. Once on a wheel you can relax physically but not mentally; a touch of wheels will cause a crash, perhaps bringing dozens of riders down.

Riding in the pack, or peloton, lets riders shelter in the slipstream of those in front.

Other road races

Criteriums are short circuit races, often around a city centre. Riders do around 60 laps. The short, twisty-turny course means that most moves are made by individual riders. There are many one-day races, which are like a single stage of a stage race. Such races favour sprinters.

Drafting is the reason that the pack, or peloton, can go faster than a lone rider. Riders in the pack take turns to ride at the front, riding a bit harder and faster than they would by themselves, safe in the knowledge that they'll soon drop back and get a chance to recover while others come through and make the pace.

This is why breakaways are usually caught – the rider or riders in the break have to work much harder. A lone rider is also at the mercy of cross-winds, whereas several riders can form an echelon, or diagonal, across the road.

Drafting is also done for a sprinter at the finish of a stage. His team members will lead him out, shielding him from the wind so he can conserve his energy, and then he'll pounce from the slipstream for the finish. Sprinters from different teams will sometimes play cat and mouse with one another, each trying to get in the other's slipstream, both to conserve energy and create the possibility of a surprise attack.

The riders

Stage racers don't all have the same job or skills. Teams are mostly made up of domestiques, riders whose job it is to help their team leader, the team's 'star player'. Increasingly, teams carry super-domestiques, who may be given chances for glory on their own. Each team has riders who excel at sprinting, climbing and time trialling. Sprinters tend to be large, powerful riders with explosive acceleration but less staying power. Climbers are small and wiry, with a better strength-to-weight ratio. Time triallists need to be capable of sustaining hard, fast riding, and are usually of more medium build.

Recent Tour de France winners have all been strong time triallists. Miguel Indurain, winner of the Tour from 1991 to 1995, was a rider who demolished the opposition in time trials and held on to his time gap for the rest of the race.

Entering a road race

Road races for ordinary people are like those described, but are shorter and slower, and team tactics are less important until you get pretty good. Contact your national cycling organization for details; membership is often mandatory if you want to take part.

Above: The sprint finish isn't as simple as it looks. The riders don't just dash for the line, they attack from behind slipstreams.

The small front wheel of the team pursuit bikes means that the riders can get closer together, improving their ability to slipstream

TRACK RACING

Track racing takes place in an arena. Riders hurtle like greyhounds round a banked track, either indoors on wood – a velodrome – or outdoors on concrete. Spectators sit round the edges and sometimes in the middle. At Six Day races, bands play, people dine, and champagne corks pop.

Riding the track

An Olympic track is nominally 333.3 metres (364 yards) long, but most tracks are 250 metres (273 yards). The banking is as steep as 50° in the bends, though it's shallower in the straights.

The banking helps riders speed up or slow down – they just go up it or swoop down it. This is important as the riders have no brakes, and can only otherwise check their speed using their cranks and the fixed gear.

Multiple gears aren't necessary on the track as there are no hills. Despite the single gear, vast speeds are achieved. The record for a one-hour time trial is over 34 mph (54.715 kh), while speeds of 50 mph (80 kh) are not unknown in sprints. Falls at these speeds can be very dangerous indeed.

Track events

The simplest track event is the time trial. Tactics are minimal: individual riders race against the clock, taking as short a route as they can around the bottom of the track. Team time trials involve teams of four riders, and are much faster because the riders draft (see Road racing page 88).

In the pursuit, two riders (or teams) start simultaneously on opposite sides of the track, then pursue one another, usually over 4km (2.5 miles), 3km (nearly 2 miles) for women and 5km (just over 3 miles) for the men's team event. The rider or team that gains the most ground, or overlaps their opponent, wins.

Sprints are more tactical. The race takes place between two riders over three laps, but only the last 200 metres (217 yards) count. The early part of the race is spent jockeying for position. Each rider wants to ride in the other's slipstream, both to save energy and to launch a surprise attack.

A points race takes place between around 20 riders over a set number of laps; 100 is common. The first riders over every fifth lap earn points, so breakaways and chases occur over every four intervening laps, rather like in a road race, and there's a hectic sprint for the line every fifth.

The madison is a kind of sprint, which uses teams of two riders. One member of each team races round the velodrome against one member

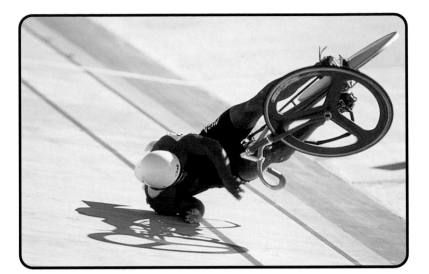

from each of the other teams, while the non-racing partners slowly circle around the top of the banking. When one of the racers tires, he signals to his partner, who comes down the banking and links hands with his team mate, who then uses his momentum to fling him up to speed and into the race.

The madison gets its name from where it originated in the early part of this century: the velodrome in Madison Square Garden, New York. It's a mainstay of Six Day races (the intense six-day track events which take place in Europe through the winter).

Above: Track bikes use tubular tyres which are stuck to the rim with special glue. These tyres rarely roll off, but when they do, the crashes are dramatic and often painful.

Track bikes

All track bikes have a single fixed gear and no brakes. Pursuit and time trial bikes are mirror images of road time trial bikes, except for the lack of brakes and gears. On an indoor track, riders can get more aerodynamic than on the road, since

the lack of crosswinds means that they can safely use a disk wheel at both the front and the rear.

Track bikes used in sprints need to be light, since it takes less time to get a smaller mass moving; they may weigh as little as 14lb (6.3kg). They also need to be stronger. Handlebars, which the riders wrench on when getting up to speed, are heavier, stronger steel rather than lighter, weaker alloys.

Wheels are spoked, but the hub flanges are bigger. This allows shorter spokes, giving the wheel greater lateral strength, which is important on a banked track. Spokes may also be tied together where they cross with thin pieces of wire, and then soldered, giving them yet more lateral stiffness.

The wheelbase of the bike is shorter, as this is better for acceleration and there's little danger of a foot hitting the front wheel, since it is only ever turned slightly; the banking helps turn the rider.

CYCLO-CROSS

Back in the 1920s, before the mountain bike was a twinkle in anybody's eye, cyclists were already racing their bikes through mud and over logs. Cyclo-cross, which is a kind of hybrid of cycling and cross-country running, has remained a popular winter sport for cyclists ever since.

Riding cyclo-cross

Cyclo-cross is very intense compared to road racing. Circuits are only about a mile long, and races last 12 or so laps. The event is all over within an hour.

Course conditions vary enormously. Most have a mix of tarmac road, grassy sections, muddy single-track, and slopes where you have to get off and run with the bike on your shoulder. Hazards like logs, ditches or even streams are worked into the circuit.

Because of the slow speed and tricky conditions, aerodynamics are almost irrelevant, so tactics play second fiddle to endurance and bike-handling skills. To do well, you need to practise riding off-road, and do cross-country running in your training. You should also try to improve the speed at which you mount and dismount the bike, because you'll be doing it often, as it's an area where time is easily lost.

Cyclo-cross is very similar to cross-country mountain bike racing – although it would be truer to say MTB cross-country is like cyclo-cross. The difference is that mountain bike courses tend to be technically harder and slower. In a mountain bike race you are also not allowed a change of bike, whereas in a 'cross race you are.

Whereas mountain bikers may try to ride tricky terrain, a cyclo-crosser will shoulder his bike and run with it.

The cyclo-cross bike

A dedicated cyclo-cross bike fits in somewhere between a stripped down tourer and a road bike. The frame angles are shallower than on a road bike to give greater stability. A 'cross bike uses a tourer's cantilever brakes, which give greater stopping power and won't clog with mud like caliper brakes.

Wheels are 700C, with fairly narrow knobbly tyres. Exact tyre width and pressure will depend on conditions at the course – fat and soft for lots of mud, thin and hard for lots of grass – but they're all thinner than most MTB tyres. Gear levers used to be bar end levers, but these days the combined brake/gear lever systems like Shimano's STI and Campagnolo's Ergopower are common.

The gears themselves are smaller across the board, reflecting the lower speeds. The cassette will have bigger sprockets than a road bike (12–26 or 13–28 is common) while the chainrings are slightly smaller. SPD pedals are used, since the recessed cleat allows easy running. Small studs are used in the shoes for extra grip.

Although most hard-core 'cross riders use bikes like this, many riders use mountain bikes, which can be successfully raced without modification. A touring bike would be easy to adapt, however; you'd just need to strip it down.

The cyclo-cross bike is more fragile than a mountain bike, but riders can switch bikes during the race; mountain bikers cannot.

Entering a race

The cyclo-cross season runs from September to February, in road cycling's off-season. Some road riders keep fit by doing 'cross in the winter, and it has to be said that it's a much more interesting way to keep fit than churning away at home on a turbo trainer.

Races can be quite informal compared to road racing. There's very little red tape and no form filling. For most races you can just turn up on the day and pay a small entry fee. All you need is a bike – what you ride is up to you – and a helmet.

RACING FOR CHILDREN

Remember how exciting it was when you rode your first bike? It was great fun. And when you have children you'll want them to discover this too. So you get them a bike. But you may consider that encouraging them to race is a bit pushy, or a bit serious. It needn't be either.

Why race?

Every child with a bike races it sometime or other – round the block against friends, or just to see how fast they can go. An organized race simply gives them a better opportunity, and usually a better environment, to go tearing around on their bike. If they win, great; if not, it doesn't matter. Racing at this level is all about taking part and enjoying the event.

You may feel you have the next Chris Boardman or John Tomac on your hands. Let it wait. Give your children the opportunity to race, and the support when they do, but let them make the decisions. If you force them to race, they may rebel and hate cycling for the rest of their lives. Better that they continue cycling and enjoy it, competitive or not.

What event?

As soon as your boy or girl can ride a bike (stabilizers don't count), they can compete, but it's probably better to wait until they're fairly confident on their bikes.

BMX and mountain bike races cater for children of all ages, and these forms of racing are a great introduction. Chances are they'll be riding the same kind of bike they learned on. And the course will be off-road, so there won't be any traffic around, and the inevitable spills will be less serious. Contact your national cycling organization or check cycling magazines for race details; it's rare you need to pre-book.

In Britain there's no lower age limit for road racing, but children can't generally cope with dropped handlebars until they're seven or eight. They can't enter a time trial in Britain until the age of 12, unless they're on the back of a tandem with an adult.

Preparation

Structured training is pointless for children below the age of puberty, and too much training can even do harm – both to the child's developing body, and to their interest in cycling.

At most, let them have a short training ride of less than an hour when they feel like it (but no more than three or four times a week). This ride should raise the heart rate, but not to the extent that they can't talk to you along the way. If they don't want to ride, fine. Just let them race.

From 14 onwards, children can try structure training, but it should be aerobic training, and only about an hour or so, three or four times a week. One race a week is fine for this age group.

Children and exercise

Throughout the western world, children are taking less and less exercise, and some pundits are predicting a generation of couch potatoes, with accompanying increases in heart disease and obesity. So if your child likes cycling, great stuff!

Children respond to aerobic exercise similar to adults, gaining endurance and lowering resting and active heart rates. However, they do not benefit from anaerobic (high intensity) training, as their bodies have low levels of key enzymes. Nor should they do resistance training (ie weight training). Resistance training isn't much use to cyclists anyway, but it can cause problems with the still growing skeleton of a child.

Far left: BMX racing is alive and well, and it caters for children of all ages.

Left: Mountain bike courses are tougher than the short BMX tracks, but are still a great way into cycle sport.

WHY CYCLING IS GOOD FOR YOU

Riding a bike isn't just fun, it's an antidote to many of the ailments that beset the modern man. If you're a regular cyclist, your chances of dying from heart disease – the western world's biggest killer – plummet. Your weight stabilizes at a healthy level. You look and feel better. You even cope with stress better. This is why the British Medical Association called on the British Government to promote cycling.

Better by bike

Any exercise is good for you, but cycling is one of the best kinds. Running stresses the ankles, knees, hips and Achilles' tendons. It's hard and it hurts – especially if you are overweight. Weightlifting builds muscles but won't make you fit.

Only swimming is better than cycling as an all-round aerobic work-out. But it's nowhere near as convenient, and can't be integrated into daily life like cycling can. You can get useful exercise on your bike by cycling to the shops. All you can do when you go swimming is swim, and you have to make a special effort (and pay money) to go and do it.

Cycling requires no special facilities, and almost no cash outlay once you have your bike. Anyone from four to 84 can participate.

Running seriously jars the joints. Cycling is a low impact sport.

A healthy heart

The heart is basically just a muscle that pumps blood, and like any muscle you can make it bigger and stronger through exercise. If you don't force it to work hard occasionally – three times a week for twenty minutes is all it takes – it will become weak. The sluggish flow of blood means that it may also start to clog, with deposits building up on the linings of the arteries like lime-scale in piping.

Your heart then strains to pump a given volume of blood. If you place demands on it – running upstairs one day, perhaps – your heart can't cope, and seizes: heart attack.

Regular exercise makes the heart into a more efficient pump, and the sluicing of the blood around the body – up from five litres a minute at rest to

Far left: Cycling is good for the mind as well as the body because it's so relaxing.

Left: Few forms of exercise beat cycling if you want to shape up your lower body. Buttocks, thighs and calves all become leaner and more muscular.

25 litres during exercise – helps keep the valves and arteries clear.

Cycling also combats the secondary causes of heart disease: high blood pressure, obesity, and stress. Exercise lowers blood pressure. Good news when you consider that men with only moderately high blood pressure stand to live about 15 years less than men with low blood pressure [1].

A better body

Cycling uses the biggest muscles in the human body, specifically the quadriceps in the upper thigh, and the gluteus maximus in the backside. The calf muscles are also used. So if you want to tone your legs, get riding.

Cycling is likely to make you fitter and leaner. Non-strenuous cycling burns up around 250-300 calories per hour. A kilogram (2lb 3oz) of body fat contains about 7,700 calories. To lose one kilo you'd have to cycle for at least 25 hours, which at half an hour a day, every day, is seven weeks.

It's not an instant weight loss scheme, but it beats starving yourself. It'll help if you also eat less fatty and sugary food. But fortunately regular cycling can actually help you regulate your appetite. Try it. If you're not overweight, you can eat more than a sedentary person without increasing your bodyweight.

Mens sana in corpore sano

'A healthy mind in a healthy body' – the Romans recognized this a couple of thousand years ago, and it's still true. It's why PE is on the school curriculum. It's why people who are glowing with health have a positive, can-do outlook on everything.

Cycling, like any exercise, is also a good antidote to stress. You go out, ride hard, and 'get it out of your system' in a way that you just can't do if you climb into a car. This makes cycling especially good for commuters: instead of cursing your way through a traffic jam, you arrive at work calm and collected, and you arrive at home refreshed. Perfect.

1 Cycling Towards Health and Safety, British Medical Association, 1992.

ACHES AND PAINS

Cycling isn't always problem free, especially when you're starting out. Here are some aches and pains you might encounter, and ways to deal with them.

PROBLEM	POSSIBLE CAUSE	CURE
Aching knees	1. Riding in too high a gear.	1. Ride in a gear that you can spin, not a gear that you have to force round. You should be able to pedal at around 90rpm. Count your pedal strokes over ten seconds then multiply by six to check.
	2. Riding with the saddle set too low.	2. Raise your saddle so that, with your heel on the pedal, your leg is fully extended. When pedalling with the ball of your foot, your leg should be almost fully extended on each pedal revolution.
	3. Your knees are cold.	3. On a cold day, wear tights, 3/4 length knicker bockers or leg warmers.
Numb/sore backside	1. Saddle tilted upwards.	1. Using a spirit level, make the top of your saddle dead level, or even tilted downwards very slightly.
	2. Saddle doesn't suit you – it's too hard, too narrow or too broad.	2. Take your bike to a shop and try some different saddles. Also be sure to wear padded cycling shorts.
	3. Riding too far too soon.	3. Increase mileage gradually.
Numb/sore feet	1. Wearing shoes with a thin and/or flexible sole.	1. Use shoes with a stiff sole, preferably cycling shoes.
	2. Wearing shoes that are too tight, or using toe clips that are too tight.	2. Use shoes with a better fit, loosen toe clips, or try riding with clipless pedals.
Lower back ache	1. Saddle too high causing pelvis to rock from side to side on each pedal stroke making vertebrae rub against each other.	1. Lower saddle so that your leg is not fully extending each pedal stroke.

Problem	Cause	Solution
Lower back ache (continued)	2. Too stretched out on bike, or too low.	2. Does the bike fit? See page 22 If it does, try raising stem. No luck? Try a shorter reach stem with more vertical adjustment.
Shoulders ache	1. Handlebars too wide.	1. Saw off ends of handlebars until they are same width as shoulders (flat bars) or buy new ones (drops).
	2. Too much weight on arms.	2. Use shorter, more upright stem. If time trialling, use tri bars
Wrists ache	1. Too much weight on arms.	1. Use shorter, more upright stem.
	2. Using same hand position on bars on a long ride.	2. Vary hand position. Use tops of bars and brake hoods on drops. With flat bars, fit bar ends and use them occasionally.
Numb/sore hands	1. Gripping bars too tightly.	1. Don't grip so hard.
	2. Insufficient padding on grips.	2. Use padded grips or padded handlebar tape, and/or padded cycling mitts.
	3. Failing to vary hand position.	3. Vary hand position (as above).
	4. Too much weight on arms.	4. As above (Wrists ache).
Stiff neck	1. Riding on drops too much or too stretched out, forcing neck to arch further to look ahead.	1. Ride on brake hoods and tops. f you need to ride on drops a lot, try shallower drops. If too stretched out, change stem.
Light-headed	1. Dehydrated.	1. Drink plenty of fluid. Drink regularly.
	2. Low blood sugar.	2. Take snacks with you on all longer rides. Energy bars or bananas are good.
Eyes water	1. Wind, sun, dust.	1. Wear sunglasses. Clear ones are available for poor light.
Cramp	1. Dehydrated.	1. Drink regularly.
	2. Riding too hard without training or stretching.	2. Build up distances gradually, and be sure to warm up by stretching or cycling gently before hard riding. If severe, take a hot bath or use spray-on muscle relaxant.
Stitch	1. Not enough oxygen getting to the muscles, possibly caused by panting.	1. Breathe deeply. Reduce speed.
Tight leg muscles	1. Not stretching.	1. Do some stretching before and after rides. Try swimming.

Prevention not cure

Be sure to set your bike up correctly. Refer to 'The Right Bike'. The stretches described below are very useful for cyclists too. Do these stretches slowly, and without pain, and hold for a count of ten. Do not 'bounce'.

Calf stretch (left).
Stand two feet from a wall, legs straight, hands flat against the wall. Lean towards the wall.

Hamstring stretch (right).
Put one foot on a table, bend over and touch your toes. Repeat for other leg.

Quad stretch.
Lie face down on the floor, grab one leg at your ankle, and pull your ankle towards your back. Repeat for the other leg.

Lower back stretch.
Lie face up, grab legs behind knees and pull them in to your chest.

EAT TO RIDE

Nutrition isn't as complicated as it's cracked up to be. Most diet books could be replaced by a single sentence: if you eat more calories than you expend, you get fat; if you eat fewer, you lose weight. Likewise, there's nothing mysterious about eating for cycling. For meals, just follow the dietary advice everyone else ought to follow: eat lots of carbohydrates, some protein and a little fat.

Above: Products like these supply a quick fix of energy but are not a substitute for a good diet.

Carbohydrate – what, how and when

Carbohydrate is the fuel on which your body runs. It's stored in your liver and muscles as a substance known as glycogen.

Good sources of carbohydrate include potatoes, pasta, rice and bread – bulk foods, basically. It's these foods that you should base meals around, and eat plenty of if you're hungry.

To be sure you have plenty of carbohydrate available for your glycogen stores, you should eat regular, square meals – including, most importantly, breakfast. Don't skip a meal then binge on chocolate.

After you have finished exercise, your body is eager to fill up on carbohydrate. Try to eat something in the two hours immediately afterwards, or you may feel tired the next day.

Fat, protein and sugar

You need some fats: olive oil, seed oils and fish oils are good; saturated animal fat is bad. You don't need lots of fat. You especially don't want lots of fat combined with sugar or protein.

Protein is what your body builds and repairs itself from. You need a regular supply, though less than you think. You don't want protein with lots of fat, and unfortunately many protein sources come freighted with fat – such as red meat and some dairy products. Better protein sources are therefore white poultry meat, fish, beans, lentils and tofu.

As a regular exerciser, sugar is not your enemy. It is an energy source. Sugar is good when it comes as fructose in fruit, and doesn't do harm (unless calories in exceed calories out, and/or you don't brush your teeth) when you have it in drinks either. Sugar is bad when it's comes wrapped in lots of fat – biscuits, chocolate, ice cream, cakes. Keep these things as treats only.

Vitamins and minerals

Eat plenty of fresh fruit and veg and you do not need to worry about vitamins, period. Vitamins you want plenty of include A, C and E. As well as keeping you in tip top condition generally, these vitamins are anti-oxidants; jargon for 'helps stop your muscles hurting after exercise'.

Vitamin A comes in green, yellow and red vegetables, including spinach, carrots, beetroot and sweetcorn. Vitamin E comes in nuts, seeds, seed oils and whole grains (eg wholemeal bread). Vitamin C comes in raw or lightly cooked vegetables, fruit, and fruit juice.

Unlike vitamin deficiency, iron deficiency is fairly common. One of the main symptoms is fatigue. You can get iron from green vegetables, dried fruit, beans, pulses and wholemeal bread. You can also get it from (lean) red meat and dark poultry meat.

Eating on the road

Cycling jerseys have pockets in the back which are useful for carrying snacks. If you're cycling any distance, you need to eat to keep your carbohydrate stores topped up. Bulky carbohydrates like potatoes are obviously out. Fat-free sugary foods are great. The banana is the traditional snack, but energy bars are even better. You can even have liquid food such as carbohydrate packed drinks.

Run out of carbohydrate stores (glycogen) and you run out of energy, and into what runners and cyclists know as The Wall. Your legs suddenly feel very heavy and you lose all of your power. Ride over.

You also need to keep your blood sugar level up. Low blood sugar brings light-headedness and poor coordination. This too can be avoided by munching on snacks as you ride.

And finally...

Anything – including chocolate – is okay as a treat. Just don't live on treats.

Above: Take snacks on any but the shortest rides. That energy bar will make all the difference when you start to tire.

Don't dehydrate

Losing as little as 2% of your bodyweight through sweat (three pints for a 150lb person) is enough to affect your performance. You can lose more than this before you become thirsty, so drink plenty and often. After rides in hot weather, weigh yourself. Lost a pound? Drink a pint of water.

RACE TRAINING

Regular cycling will keep you pretty healthy, but it won't turn you into an athlete. If you want to race and do well you'll need to do more specific training than riding to the shops.

Training levels

To train effectively it helps to know what your maximum heart rate is (also known as threshold heart rate). As a rough guide, you can find this by subtracting your age from 220. You can get a more precise idea by going out and riding a ten-mile time trial (or just riding ten miles as fast as you can) while wearing a pulse monitor. The level you peak and keep at is your maximum heart rate.

When you have calculated your maximum heart rate, you can work out your appropriate pulse for the four training levels which sports scientists use. Your pulse rate gives you an indication of the calories you are burning, and therefore the energy you are expending, while cycling.

Pulse monitor

A pulse monitor is probably the most useful training aid for anyone wanting to get fit. Basic models from Polar and Cardiosport

level **2**

Level One

More than 30 beats below your maximum heart rate.

This equates to easy riding, where you don't get out of breath and can chat normally. Riding at this level won't make you much fitter, since your heart rate does not rise by much, but it's useful for warming up and warming down.

level **1**

Level Two

10–15 beats below your maximum heart rate.
At this level you can still talk, albeit with more difficulty, and you have to keep your mind on maintaining your pace. You should be able to keep this up for around three hours. This level of training should make up the bulk of your training schedule.

Level Three

At your maximum heart rate.
This is the level you hit in a 10-mile time trial.

aren't too expensive. All you really need is the pulse display, though the ability to record your pulse reading is also useful. Some models have alarms that beep if your pulse drops above or below a certain level.

The position on recovery

Constant training won't make you a better cyclist. You only get better when you stop – that is, when you take time off to recover. Training works by stressing your body, which stimulates it to make itself stronger. By pushing your body beyond what it is used to, you force it to overcompensate, to get fitter! But it takes time – meaning rest – for your body to adapt to these new stresses.

You must also eat and drink plenty during and after training. Beware over-training. If you feel tired when you climb on your bike, get off it, have something to eat, and go and have a lie down. Try later.

Your first training schedule

First devise a route, preferably without any enormous hills, that takes you about an hour to ride. Ride this three or four times a week, on alternate days. Don't push it to begin with: ride somewhere between Level One and Level Two (30–15 beats below maximum heart rate).

After a week or two, start riding the route at Level Two (10–15 beats below maximum heart rate). Note that you'll now be finishing the route rather more quickly.

After a couple of weeks of riding your route at Level Two, look to increase the length of some of your rides. Go out for two hours – perhaps at the weekend – at just below Level Two, then go up to Level Two for this particular ride.

Add in another two-hour, Level Two ride when you feel ready, so that your training schedule looks something like this:

Sunday:	Level Two, 2 hours
Monday:	Rest
Tuesday:	Level Two, 1 hour before or after work
Wednesday:	Rest
Thursday:	Level Two, 1 hour before or after work
Friday:	Rest
Saturday:	Level Two, 2 hours

Keep this up for a couple of months and you're ready for your first time trial. Go for it! And see how the time compares to the one you did to find you maximum heart rate a few months earlier in the programme.

The next step, if you haven't already, is to join a cycling club. Fellow club members, cycling magazines and specific training books will help you develop your training schedule further.

level **3**

You can't talk as you must breathe deeply and regularly. It's very effective at training your body, but you can only keep it up for about half an hour at most.

Level Four
Above your maximum heart rate.
At this level you are exercising anaerobically (ie not using oxygen to fuel your muscles). You can only ride like this in short bursts. Riding at this level is useful for sprint training.

level **4**

MAINTENANCE

DIY or call the experts?

Some people would have you believe that anything mechanical is out of bounds to the beginner, but with the right tools for the job, some good information and a little patience you can cut down on expensive maintenance bills from the local bike shop.

As you gain experience and confidence on the small jobs you'll soon be itching for a bigger challenge…though you may need to invest in some specialist tools if you want to tackle jobs involving hubs, chains and sprockets.

Tools of the trade

All bikes need to be kept clean and well lubed (see page 112). It's worth investing in the right products from the start.

Don't rush into a job without the right tools. A loose fitting spanner or the wrong screwdriver can make a mess of a bolt or screw. Spanners have their size stamped on them – so make sure you use the right one. Extra care is needed when using cross headed screwdrivers as they're not always marked for size. For most jobs you'll need to use metric spanners, though some older bikes may require imperial spanners.

Once you have found the right spanner, make sure you turn it in the right direction. Right hand threads tighten with a clockwise turn and left hand threads tighten with an anti-clockwise turn. Cross threads can be expensive and dangerous, so don't force the thread. Starting a bolt or nut onto a thread should be a simple thumb and forefinger affair without excessive force. Particular care needs to be exercised when fitting a bottom bracket unit – if you force the cups grease is displaced and the unit corrodes, often becoming difficult to remove. A special bottom bracket thread chasing tool is available but they are too expensive for DIY maintenance.

Lubrication

Take time to keep your bike well greased. Sliding fit parts – like the seatpost and stem – can sieze up and get stuck. Apply grease to the facing parts to avoid this sticky situation.

Be careful with that oil can. Too much oil will attract dirt causing wear, especially to the chain. Too little oil will let corrosion get a hold and cause sluggish gear changes.

A multiple-use tool has all you need in one neat package – carry one wherever you ride.

Don't be tempted to spray oil into components with bearings like hubs, headset and bottom bracket – you will dilute the grease leading to the rapid wear of the components.

Know your limitations

Don't be afraid to ask – if you are unsure ask someone who knows. Bike shops are busiest during the weekend so it's better to pick a brain during the week. Staff at good bike shops will be happy to help – if they're rude, shop elsewhere.

Wheel building and trueing is probably the hardest job you'll encounter so get the help of an established wheel builder – especially if you're off touring.

Specialist tools such as these are required for removal of worn bottom brackets and other essential components.

A workstand is a useful and time saving aid for many maintenance chores.

ESSENTIAL TOOLS

A good tool kit will save you money in bike shop charges and you'll learn the art of bicycle maintenance into the bargain. The tools you'll need most are for roadside repairs and to fix punctures.

Roadside tool kit

All experienced cyclists carry a few select tools whenever they go out for a ride. A good roadside tool kit should include everything you need to repair a puncture, fix common problems (ie broken spokes, broken chain, etc.) and get you home! Make sure your kit includes the following:

Pump: Get a decent pump, preferably one with an aluminium body and chuck – it'll last longer and won't let you down. A mini pump is ideal for bikes where space is taken up with water bottle cages; frame fit pumps are convenient and widely used on road bikes. As the name suggests they fit on the frame – usually under the top tube.

Your roadside tool kit should be lightweight and contain all you need to fix common problems and get you home. Check your kit regularly – tools rust and parts perish.

Spare inner tube: Don't stand around waiting for repairs to dry, carry a spare and do your repairs at home.

Puncture repair kit: Take a puncture kit, it's good insurance in case you puncture more than once. Avoid using tyre levers unless absolutely nessesary as it's easy to nip the tube with them. Make sure your puncture repair kit includes a piece of emery cloth or sandpaper.

Multi tool: Multi tools, such as the Cool Tool, take up less space than separate tools and some include a chain rivet extractor which is essential for road and trailside repairs. An absolute must for the MTB racer.

Adjustable spanner: If your budget won't run to a multi tool, the crescent-shaped jaws of the adjustable wrench are more reliable than a cheap metal box spanner. The 6in (152mm) size will handle all the nuts on your bicycle.

Piece of wire or cable ties: Handy to bind things together in an emergency.

Spoke key: Essential for long tours. If a spoke breaks, the rim will wobble affecting control. A spoke key will allow you to loosen the remaining spokes enough to stabilize the wheel. Some tourists tape a spare spoke to the chainstay and replace broken spokes on the roadside.

The home tool kit

The list of tools available for the home workshop is huge…and growing all the time. However the following tools should equip you to carry out most everyday repairs.

Vice: Though not essential, the bench mounted vice is like an extra pair of hands. Excellent for tricky jobs like hub overhauls.

Crank extractor: You need to remove the crank arms, to change the bottom bracket.

Allen keys: The sizes you'll need most are 5mm, 6mm, 8mm and 10mm. It's worth having spares of the 5mm and 6mm keys as they're the most commonly used and also most commonly lost!

Chain rivet extractor: Essential for changing a worn chain or freeing up a stiff link.

Headset spanners: Most road bikes use the 32mm size; MTBs using 'oversized' headsets use the 36mm size. You won't, of course, need these if your headset is the threadless type (see page 166 for maintenance details).

Pin and ring spanners

The pin spanner has a pair of adjustable pins which engage the holes in a bearing cup, enabling it to be held while the locking ring is tightened. A ring spanner is used to fix a threaded ring such as the locking ring on an adjustable cup.

Essentials

Carry this tool kit and you'll be ready for anything…almost.
• Chainsplitter and spare links
• Inner tube
• Allen keys
• 3 longish cable ties or solid copper wire (both available from electrical wholesalers)
• Spoke key
(A multi purpose tool can replace many of the above)

If you want to look after your bike properly, it's worth investing in the right tools. Nowadays there's a growing number of specialist parts with tools to go with them.

PRE-RIDE CHECKS

Grade of job: Easy.

It's easier to fix your bike at home than the roadside. And if you're riding with friends, they won't thank you for breaking down and spoiling the ride. So check your bike before you set off.

Give the tyres a quick squeeze before the ride. If in doubt top them up with air and check the pressure with a gauge.

1. Tyres:
Don't expect your tyres to be how you left them. Inner tubes loose air gradually and need topping up to between 40–50psi for MTBs, and around 100psi for road bikes. Follow the makers recommendation for exact pressures.

2. Brake pads:
Release the straddle wire and inspect the blocks for wear; some brands have wear limit marks. Take into account the rigours of the ride to come and if the pads will be useless at the end of the ride, change them.

3. Brake levers:
Squeeze the brake levers hard – if they touch the bars/grips you need to improve the cable tension. If your brakes have barrel adjusters, turn them anti-clockwise. If you don't have barrel adjusters, you'll have to tighten the cables.

4. Tyre tread:
Inspect the treads of road tyres carefully for tiny fragments of glass and flints which could cut through to the inner tube. Check MTB tyre sidewalls for abrasions caused by brake blocks. Your safety depends on good tyres – replace them if they're worn.

5. Chain:
Check for stiff chain links (especially if the bike is new) by back-pedalling the cranks and watching the chain as it passes through the rear mech. Use a chain checker to gauge wear on a used chain.

6. Wheels and spokes:
Lift and spin each wheel. If the brakes rub, check there are no broken spokes – they usually break at the hub end. Now, true the wheel (see page 122)

7. Saddle:
If your saddle has dropped at the nose, remove the bolt or nut and apply a little grease to the bolt thread. Tighten the bolt or nut using a ring spanner. Check the saddle height and mark the seatpost with a pen – this makes it easy to set the saddle at the same height if you have to remove it.

8. Headset:
Apply the front brake and rock the bike forward and back, if there's play go to page 166 (headsets).

9. Wheels tight:
It's essential to be familiar with the correct way to operate a quick release skewer. It is secured by turning in a clockwise direction until it is reasonably tight, then adjusting the lever position, using the nut on the other side, so that it's in line with the wheel axle. The lever should then be pressed home using the palms of your hands.

TIP
> Save time on pre-ride checks with a track pump - they make inflating a tyre easy and most have a built-in pressure gauge. A gauge cuts out uncertainty, so if you don't want to carry a track pump with you a pressure gauge may be a worthwhile investment.

If the levers pull back this far, the cable needs adjusting.

Make sure wheels are tight. Quick release skewers turn clockwise.

Lift and spin the wheels to check they are running true.

Quick release levers should be tightened using the palm of the hand.

AFTER RIDE CARE

Grade of job: Very easy.

After a ride get to grips with cleaning your bike – even if your excursion didn't include a ride through the mud. This doesn't mean stopping at the nearest garage and blasting the bike with a jet wash. These machines operate at such high pressure that water could penetrate the bearing seals. What you should do is...

1. Fill a large bucket with warm water and a little washing-up liquid. Using a washing-up brush, and starting from the underside of the saddle, work down the bike gently running the brush over the whole bike. Flip off the brake straddle wire and run a screwdriver through the gaps in the brake blocks to remove small stones. If mud has dried on the tyres, run the wet brush over them, let it soak in and return to them later.

2. Using a separate brush or a chain-cleaning device, apply a solvent cleaner to the chain, sprockets and chain rings. Leave the solvent for about 10 minutes to melt the grime.

3. Return to the tyres – the water you applied earlier will have softened the mud by now. Rinse off with water and clean the spokes and hubs.

4. Run the washing-up brush along the chain and scrub between the rear wheel sprockets and chain rings using plenty of water. Ensure that there's no mud left on the derailleurs before liberally spraying the moving parts and the chain with a water dispersant, such as WD40, to expel moisture, pay particular attention to cables where moisture can lurk. Wipe off any excess dispersant with a rag then apply a heavy mineral oil or an effective spray lube.

If you must use a jet-wash to clean your bike, first protect the bearings with a rag.

After you've cleaned the chain, spray it with a water dispersant such as WD40, then wipe the chain clean with a rag and re-lube.

TIP
> If you haven't got a drain hole in your frame (see Looking after your frame, page 164) lift the seatpost and invert the bike to drain off any water that has accumulated during the ride.

Worn brake blocks are extremely dangerous. Check them regularly for signs of wear. Badly aligned brake blocks will wear most quickly so keep them well-aligned.

LUBRICATION

Moving parts need lubrication to keep running smoothly, but different parts require different lubes. Many components have seals these days, but they are only partially effective and become less so if you ride without mudguards. With extended use, the grease within the parts displaces leaving bearings exposed and susceptible to corrosion if left unchecked. How and when you lube your bike depends on the type of riding you do. If you ride off road it's best to re-lube the whole bike after a wet, muddy ride.

1. Shimano and Campagnolo hubs must be serviced periodically using a waterproof grease. Carefully remove cartridge bearing dust caps and squeeze a little Lithium-based grease into the bearings.

2. The brake and gear cables require a light mineral oil or a lube containing Teflon Oil them after every wet ride off road and every 4–6 months on road bikes.

3. Gear levers such as GripShift require special silicon grease every four months or after two very wet rides off road. These are the only shifters that require lubrication.

4. Most headsets require servicing using a waterproof grease, especially following several rides off road in wet conditions. Road bikes fitted with mudguards can be greased annually.

5. Black resin-bodied pedals with clips and straps are very susceptible to corrosion and should be greased after every wet ride. Spray the outer parts of pedals such as Shimano SPD with a spray oil.

6. Most MTBs have sealed non-serviceable bottom bracket units though older style units require fresh grease every six months. Your dealer will be able to identify the type of bottom bracket you have.

7. Use a lube containing Teflon on the front and rear gear mech pivots and the control cables which serve them.

8. Apply grease or anti-seize compound to the seatpost to prevent corrosion.

9. Use a 'dry' lube on the chain and ancillary items such as chain tensioning devices and jockey wheels; they're less susceptible to picking up dust than mineral oil.

10. Re-lube the cantilever brake bosses using waterproof grease.

11. Use penetrating oil or a water displacing spray oil on stiff spoke nipples and leave overnight before trying to adjust spoke tension.

GET YOU HOME TIPS

With improvisation these 'get you home' tips can salvage a day's riding. It is essential to take a pump everywhere and to replace the spare inner tube you used last time you had a 'flat'. Here are the seven most frequently encountered problems and their answers.

1. Fork and frame bent at the junction of the head and down tubes.

Remove the wheel and get a friend (the heavier the better) to stand on the forks – alternatively fit the fork blades into the slots of a drain cover. Grab hold of the chain stays and use your body weight to bend the frame back into shape once more.

Time – 10–20 mins.

Grade of difficulty – Moderate.

2. The rear mech catches in a rock bending it badly.

Grasp the cageplate and bend it back with your hands until straight. You'll find the cageplate easier to lever using a screwdriver. Adjust the mech to avoid clashing with the spokes in first gear.

Time – 20–30 mins.

Grade of difficulty – Moderate.

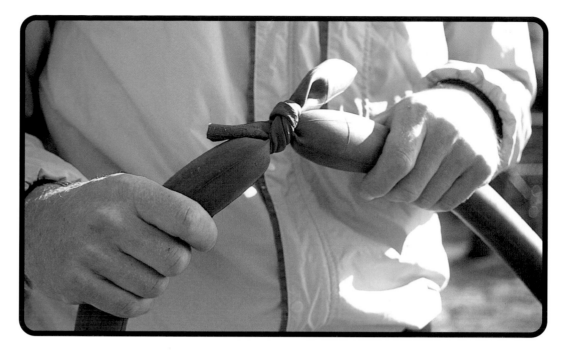

3. The tyre has exploded and the tube has a lovely big hole in it.
Cut the inner tube where it's blown then tie the ends together in a square knot. Inflate to 50psi and avoid gnarly descents for the rest of the day. Don't forget to replace both tyre and tube when you get home!
Time – 20–30 mins.
Grade of difficulty – Moderate.

4. A buckled wheel.
Place the wheel against a wall or a rock at a 45-degree angle and apply pressure to the sides of the rim until the wheel is straight again. The slot of a drain cover is a good way to refine your handywork.
Time – 15–30 mins.
Grade of difficulty – Hard.

5. Flat tyre and pump lost/broken.
Remove the inner tube and stuff the tyre as tightly as you can with grass or hay. Proceed with care especially when negotiating bends.
Time – depends where you are!
Grade of difficulty – Easy.

6. The jockey wheel falls off and is lost.
Remove the upper-most jockey wheel and fit where the lower one was, run on the large chainring and avoid changing gear.
Time – 15–20 mins.
Grade of difficulty – Moderate.

continued over

7. Rear wheel pulled over and you've lost your spanners.
Use your palms to force the wheel straight in the dropouts then select a small gear. Find a piece of fencing wire and a small stick. Wind the wire around the stick, then wind the wire several times around the track nut. Using the stick as a lever, place it against the side of the nut to tighten it.
Time – 30 mins.
Grade of difficulty – Hard.

8. A broken chain caused by sideplates splaying.
Shorten the chain a couple of links. If you don't have a chain tool, place a piece of fencing wire through the side plate. Use a small gear or ratchet the pedals if it grinds through the gear mechs.
Time – 10–15 mins.
Grade of difficulty – Moderate.

9. A lost bolt.
Bolts holding essential items like rack or mudguards can be replaced by bolts holding non-essential items such as a water bottle cage.
Time – 5–10 mins.
Grade of difficulty – Easy.

10. Broken spoke and replacement doesn't fit.
If the spoke is broken at the elbow, thread the new spoke through the flange and line it up with what's left of the original. Bend the old spoke half way at right angles, then loosen the nipple by about four turns. Bend the new spoke at the point that the other is bent, then twist them together. Tension the spoke using a spoke key.
Time – 30 mins – 1hr.
Grade of difficulty – Hard.

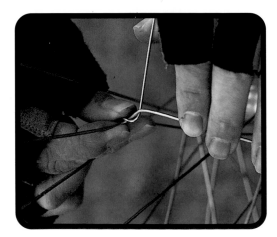

11. Twisted forks.
Twist back into shape by holding the wheel between your thighs and turning the handlebars in the appropriate direction. Look for cracks in the down tube before riding.
Time – 1–3 mins.
Grade of difficulty – Moderate.

12. Loose bottom bracket.
Italian-threaded bottom brackets habitually come loose. In the case of the cartridge units, if the right-hand cup works itself loose, the left-hand crank may become jammed against the cup. Turning the cup clockwise will temporarily free the crank arm – allowing you to proceed with the ride.
Time – 5–10 mins.
Grade of difficulty – Fairly hard.

Mission impossible
1. If you're riding in bad weather or your clothing is wet you are at risk of exposure so don't stand around fiddling to get your bike working – walk it to the nearest habitation.
2. Squeaking sounds emitting from the bottom bracket are usually a result of loose crank bolts. Continued use in this state will render the cranks useless. Walk home with the bike or tighten the crank bolts at the earliest opportunity.

WHEELS

There are as many variations of bicycle wheel as there are bicycles. The most common sizes are 26in, 27in and 700C. These sizes fit the design of the diamond frame and are large enough to absorb road surface irregularities. They also provide a balanced feel to steering which is usually lacking in the case of smaller wheels.

Whatever its size, the strength of a wheel is dependent on the number and tension of the spokes. An expertly built wheel shouldn't go out of true under normal circumstances, although an occasional turn of the spoke key will ensure that the spokes stay tight.

Time trial racing wheels

Minimum air disturbance is the priority. Aero wheels, so called as they have an aerodynamic shape, have a pointed profile that cuts through the air. They are made from aluminum or carbon fibre and often have spokes with a bladed profile to help increase aerodynamics. They are expensive wheels.

Massed start racing wheels

Road racing wheels are stronger than time trial wheels as they are likely to be ridden over drain covers and potholes. In most cases they have 32 spokes – although an extra four spokes is preferable for riders weighing over 200lb (90kg). Rims are almost always aluminium.

Touring wheels

Reliability is everything. The heavy loads and poorly surfaced roads encountered on a tour require stronger wheels than those for racing. MTB 26in and 700C wheels are popular for touring. Traditionalists go for 36-spoke wheels and box section rims.

Time trial wheels cut through the air more efficiently than standard spoked wheels. They use tubular tyres which are glued to the rim.

The larger 700C touring wheel has 36 stainless steel spokes and tyres designed to carry heavy loads. By contrast, the smaller wheel has a fat tyre and is taken from a folding bike.

MTB racing wheels

These have lighter rims and thinner spokes than those used for touring. A 32-spoke wheel is light and strong. A 36-hole rim is used for downhill racing where strength is more important than low weight.

Spokes

Spokes are arranged in a crossed pattern. The most popular pattern for spoking is 'three cross' – each spoke is crossed by three others. Radial spoking (where no spokes cross over), saves a few grams but is prone to loosening and puts a strain on the hub flange.

Tyre treads

A tyre with tread creates friction to maintain grip. This is valuable in wet conditions and is beneficial to tourists and recreational cyclists. The smooth surface on competition tyres gives a lower rolling resistance than a tyre with a tread. But it's a straightforward trade off: less rolling resistance means less grip.

Mountain bikes are often supplied with a knobbly tread. If you do most of your riding on the road, changing these for a smooth tread tyre will significantly lower the rolling resistance of the bike. A set of slick tyres is the best upgrade you can make to an MTB for road use.

Hard or soft compounds

Soft rubber works better than hard compounds in the wet. Dual compound treads are popular on road bikes. They have a hard compound centre tread for longevity and a softer compound on the tyre's edge for cornering.

Soft rubber tyres work well off-road too. They are most suitable for riding on wet grass and slippery rocks where hard rubber can cause sudden slides.

Kevlar, the material used for bullet-proof vests, is also employed in puncture-resistant tyres. It resists intrusions for longer than other materials so the intrusion is less likely to pierce the casing. Kevlar is also used on the sidewall to resist tearing.

Above: Lightly roughen the affected area.

Right: If you're using glue, make sure it's touch dry before applying the patch.

PUNCTURE REPAIRS AND TYRES

Grade of job: Easy.
Tools: Your hands!
Time: A couple of minutes.

Get the correct size tyre

The markings on a tyre sidewall are to an internationally recognized stardard called ISO – there are two numbers (eg 37–622). The first number refers to the section of the tyre, the second is the bead diameter in mm. An imperial equivalent is often shown. Make sure you know what size tyre you need before asking your shop for a replacement.

Tyre widths vary greatly. MTB tyres are available in sizes up to 2.3in wide. A tyre like this offers a shock absorbant aspect needed for the rigours of off-road riding. By contrast road race bikes need to cheat the wind with narrow tyres. A 20mm tyre is popular, though 25mm tyres, which provide greater comfort for long spells in the saddle, are the popular choice of many cycle tourists.

The markings on your tyre sidewall should tell you all you need to know about your tyre. In most cases recommended pressures and dimensions are clearly displayed.

Left, below and main picture: Fit one side of the tyre over the well of the rim and work the bead of the tyre over the rim using your thumbs.

Get the pressure right

Tyres lose air, so be prepared to inflate. Latex tyres are particularly prone to go down between rides as they are porous. Give your tyres a squeeze before you go for a ride and...if in doubt check their pressure with a gauge. Be careful not to exceed the recommended limit, and always follow the manufacturer's suggested pressure.

Puncture repairs

Puncture repairs are straightforward if they're due to an intrusion such as a thorn, but those caused by impact – sometimes called a pinch flat – are difficult, if not impossible, to repair. Here's how to identify a no-hoper and fit a new inner tube.

1. The inner tube has a snakebite puncture and is beyond repair. It's been caused by the tube compressing into the rim. Latex tubes, however, are almost always repairable.

2. Remove the tyre and tube then carefully inspect the bed of the rim for sharp objects and any protruding spokes. Replace the rim tape if it's damaged.

3. Fit one side of the tyre over the well of the rim. Inflate the tube so that it's firm, then place the valve through the hole.

4. Working from waist height downwards, work the bead of the tyre over the rim using your thumbs.

5. Use your thumbs to manipulate the tyre over the inner tube.

6. Inflate the tyre to seat the bead. Do this slowly and check that the tyre bead isn't bulging out anywhere.

7. Finally, inflate to the recommended pressure.

TIPS

> It's okay to use a Presta valve in a rim which has been drilled for a Schraeder (car type) valve.

> If you are getting ready for a race it's as well to inspect the inner tube, as an unstuck patch can wreak havoc on your chances.

> If you were riding fast at the time of the puncture, examine the sidewall of the tyre for damage.

WHEEL TRUING AND SPOKE REPLACEMENT

Grade of job: Moderate.
Tools: Spoke key, Flat blade screwdriver, Freeing oil, Marker pen (optional)

The first indications that a wheel's spokes are at the end of their service life is when several break – often at the same time. In this instance you are better off investing in a new wheel or getting the wheel re-spoked with new stainless steel spokes. A true wheel gives a safe regular surface for the brake blocks to contact and remains stable at speed. Here's how to check and true up your wheels.

1. Remove the wheel and check that there is no freeplay in the axle. If there is you will be unable to true the wheel properly. See page 128 for hub adjustment details.
2. Remove the tyre, tube and rim tape and fit the wheel onto the bike or a wheel jig. If you don't have a jig, arrange pointers on the chain stays using a piece of spoke and Blutak. If you're only truing the wheel go straight to figure 4.
3. If a spoke is broken – take it to your bike shop for them to get an exact replacement. If a spoke goes on the rear wheel, you'll have to remove the cassette or freewheel before you can do this (see page 148 – Cassettes).
4. Oil the thread of the spoke and thread it through, following the existing pattern. It's okay to bow the spoke but avoid bending it too much. Fit the nipple and scew it until it just brings the spoke into the same tension as the others.
5. Using your thumbs, bend the elbow of the spoke to bring it in line with the others. If you are replacing one spoke it's unlikely that further truing will be needed. If further truing is needed see below.
6. Working your way round the wheel from the valve hole, turn the spokes ¼ of a turn on

Above: Use a bent spoke and Blutack as pointers.

Right: Thread the new inward facing spoke under the first two spokes and once over the third.

Turn spoke keys clockwise to tension spokes. Take care not to tighten them so much that the wheel can't be trued.

each revolution. If the wheel is egg-shaped it's because a group of spokes are pulling more than another group of spokes. Loosen the spokes that are squeezing the wheel into an egg shape and tighten the others. Do this gradually until the wheel takes on a round shape, then work on correcting any lateral movement.

7. Viewed from above, observe the points at which the rim touches the pointers and mark them with a pen. If the rim moves to the left, turn the spoke which is adjacent to the wobble and serves that side of the wheel, in an anticlockwise direction; then turn the two adjacent spokes serving the other side of the wheel in a clockwise direction in order to equalise the tension between left and right serving spokes.

8. If you are building a new wheel, make sure the spokes exit the flange without bowing outwards. Press them with your thumbs to straighten them out. Finally, stretch and seat the spokes by grasping opposing pairs of spokes and draw them together using your thumbs and finger.

TIPS

> Spokes should be tight, but not so tight that the rim becomes impossible to true up. If in doubt ask the advice of a reputable cycle shop.

> Nipples have a right-hand thread – they are therefore tightened by turning in a clockwise direction.

> Use an old pair of forks as a jig – spring them apart.

> Get the correct type of spoke – a plain gauge spoke is the same thickness along its whole length. A double-butted spoke has a thin centre section and is thicker at each end.

As part of your regular maintenance checks, keep the spokes tight using the correct spoke key for your bike.

FRONT AND FREEWHEEL TYPE REAR HUBS

Grade of job: Difficult.
Tools: Centre punch, Hammer, Protective eye wear.

Rear hubs

Cassette hubs have replaced the screw on freewheel on most bikes though many cheaper bikes still have a freewheel. The threaded hub can be immediately identified by the fact that there's no outer locking ring to retain the smallest sprocket. The advantage with a freewheel is that it can be taken apart to replace the bearings and, unlike a freehub, it can be oiled easily. Both types of hub use an axle and ball bearings; however those on the threaded hub are narrower between the bearings and thus more prone to wear. The sequence for inspecting the bearings of a threaded hub is the same as for a freehub, but we recommend checking the axle for roundness as they are prone to bending.

Servicing a freewheel

A freewheel as opposed to a freehub is a user maintainable item. Worn bearings in the freewheel will accelerate wear and affect the way the gears operate. To replace the bearings follow the six easy steps below.

Freewheels are available in either close or wide ratio. Close ratio hubs tend to be favoured by road racers, whereas wider ratios are the popular choice for most MTBs and touring bikes.

Right, top: Specially designed hubs are required for use with supension forks.

Right, bottom: This silver hub is lightweight and suited to use on road racing bikes.

JARGON BUSTER

PAWLS: the teeth which engage within the freewheel or freehub when it's turned in a clockwise direction.
BLOCK: the freewheel.

1. Leave the freewheel on the wheel, and with it facing towards you, place the point of a small centre punch into the right hand of the two holes on the face of the freehub. Hit the punch with a short sharp blow. The ring will loosen in a clockwise direction. Always wear protective eyewear when using a hammer

2. Place the palm of your hand over the freewheel and turn the wheel to a horizontal position and place on the ground. The bearings and tiny pawls with their springs will fall out. Be careful not to lose the pawls as they aren't replaccable.

3. Inspect the bearing tracks of the freewheel for excessive wear. If they're cupped or badly pitted, replace the whole freewheel as there will be play in the unit even with new ball bearings.

4. Using grease to hold the bearings in place, fill up the bearing tracks of each side of the sprocket. Fit the pawls and their springs. Use a piece of cotton to hold the pawls down over the springs.

5. Place the sprocket assembly over the threaded centre section, and be careful not to dislodge any ball bearings as you do so. Then place any circular shims over the centre section followed by the locking ring which tightens in an anti-clockwise direction. Use the centre punch and hammer to tighten the locking ring.

6. Check that the freewheel turns smoothly and without resistance. If there is excessive freeplay in the block, you will need to remove the locking ring and lift one of the tiny thin shims from the freewheel body. Grease the thread on the hub, then screw the block over the wheel in a clockwise direction. Fit to the bike.

Front hubs

Servicing the front hub is much the same as it is for the rear, except for the fact that most ball and axle front hubs have ³⁄₁₆in (4.76mm) ball bearings, ten on each side. See page 126 for adjustment details.

NON-CARTRIDGE FREEHUBS

Grade of job: Moderate to hard.
Tools: Shimano lockring remover, Large adjustable spanner, 10mm Allen key, 14/15mm cone spanners.

Moisture penetration and subsequent corrosion is the biggest factor determining the life span of a hub – so strip and regrease your hubs to extend their life. The freehub body – the sealed unit which holds the sprockets – is attached to the main part of the hub. If the freehub feels rough when you turn the sprockets the chance is that the bearings have rusted and the freehub body needs replacing. It's quite straightforward to remove but you will need some special tools.

When you remove a cassette take great care to place the loose sprockets and locking ring in a safe place.

Stripping a Shimano hub

1. Place the left side of the wheel on the ground then remove the axle. Hold both cone spanners in the palm of one hand. Squeeze them together to loosen the locknut and cone. Remove the bearings and clean the hub's bearing surfaces and the cones with a rag. If the left-hand bearing cup surfaces are pitted throw the hubs away. If all is well, go straight to point three below.

2. Remove the cassette (see page 148 – Cassettes).
   Insert a 10mm Allen key into the freehub end of the hub, and turn it anti-clockwise to remove it. Replace it with the same make and model of freehub.

3. Fit the replacment freehub and carefully screw on the hollow fixing bolt. If it's a tight fit, you've crossed the thread.

4. If the cones show any sign of pitting renew them. Always use new bearings – the cost is small and they'll prolong the life of the hub. You'll need nine ¼in bearings for a Shimano rear hub and ten ³⁄₁₆in bearings per side for a front hub.

5. Grease the hub cups, using plenty to hold the ball bearings in place.

6. Using a vice to grip the locknut, make sure the right-hand cone is tight on the axle, then place it through the hub. Turn the left-hand cone onto the axle followed by the appropriate spacers and the locknut. Using a cone spanner and a spanner, adjust the bearings so that there is just detectable play.

TIPS

> The stainless balls on some hubs are less prone to damage than carbon-steel balls, so re-use them if they're okay.
> Always press the outer edge of a cartridge bearing into the hub, not the inner race.

Below: When you replace a freehub, check the plastic spoke protector, and replace it if it is coming loose.

Above: To remove an old freehub, turn the retaining bolt within the freehub body, in an anti-clockwise direction.

Below: To remove the axle from a freehub you will need a pair of cone spanners.

> Shimano narrow-bodied hubs (that don't have the word Parallax stamped on them), and any sealed bearing hub which has suspect seals will benefit from the fitting of 'Kak Guards', available from good cycle shops.

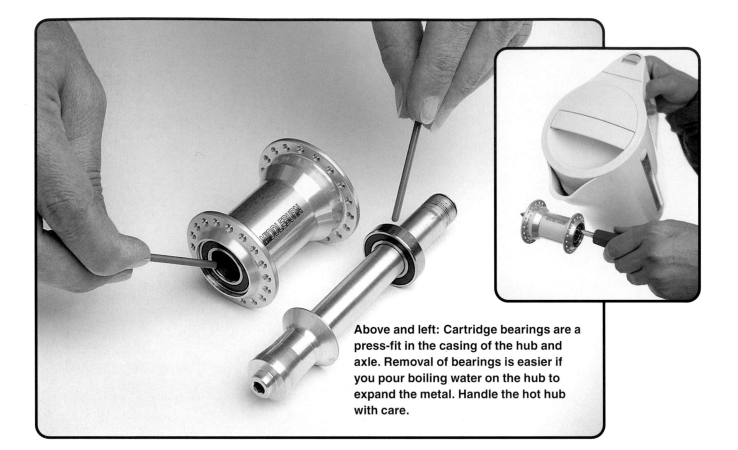

Above and left: Cartridge bearings are a press-fit in the casing of the hub and axle. Removal of bearings is easier if you pour boiling water on the hub to expand the metal. Handle the hot hub with care.

CARTRIDGE BEARING HUBS

Grade of job: Difficult.
Tools: 1.5mm or 2mm Allen wrench,
Soft-faced hammer,
Special cartridge bearing tools or
appropriate socket (around 17–19 mm)

Replacing a cartridge bearing hub

Cartridge bearing hubs are lighter than conventional hubs and contain industrial quality cartridge bearings which are adjusted at the factory. This saves weight as there's no need for an adjuster.

The downside is that it's difficult to apply fresh grease to the bearings as they're often supplied with weather seals. Corrosion can get the better of them once the grease displaces…though their worst enemy is the misdirected jetwash.

1. Try this test on both cartridge and conventional hubs. Lift the bike off the ground and spin each wheel in turn. Check for a clearly detectable rumble which is felt through the frame tubes.

2. Lift the wheel from the frame and remove the quick release. The tell-tale sign of a greaseless/dry/broken hub is if the axle will spin between thumb and forefinger without resistance. A worn cartridge bearing hub feels rough and develops play if left unchecked.

3. Cartridge bearing hubs are dismantled by removing the left hand spacer using a 1.5 mm Allen grub screw. Pull the freehub off and look after the three pawls and their coil springs. Use a soft-face hammer to tap the axle through the hub. The left-hand bearing will come out with the axle.

4. To remove a cartridge bearing from the axle, open the jaws of a vice so the axle is a sliding fit or use an adjustable spanner to hold the cartridge, and strike the axle with a soft-faced hammer to remove the bearing.

5. Use a socket to press the new bearings into the hub. It helps to warm the hubs first with boiling water to expand the metal – wear gloves when doing this to avoid burns.

6. To refit the cartridge follow the above sequence in reverse.

Above and right:
Always consult the manufacturer's instructions before fitting new bearings. A soft faced hammer is being used to remove the axle from the hub and to fit the new bearings.

TIPS

> Follow the correct sequence for installing the bearings - if you're not sure contact the supplier for literature.

> Campagnolo and Hope cassette hubs have tiny freehub pawls and springs - be careful not to lose them when you remove the freehub.

> Prise off a cartridge bearing seal to apply fresh grease to the bearings. Use a blunt knife and remove it from the outside edge; not the lip of the seal. Press fresh grease well in and use a lithium-based grease.

LACING A WHEEL

Grade of job: Difficult.
Tools: Spoke nipple key, Small screwdriver,
Wheel truing jig (optional), Wheel dishing tool (optional)

Wheel building can look like a daunting prospect but it is possible. The thing to remember is that there are two sets of spokes – the pulling ones, which drag the rim round, and the pushing spokes, which face the opposite way to the direction of rotation.

Spoke holes are angled for the left and right hub so you need to establish which spoke to put in first. It's a popular idea that the outboard spokes handle the pulling, so they need to go in after the inboard or pushing spokes.

Lacing a wheel – the key steps

1. Place the inboard spokes through alternate spoke holes on the drive side of the hub.
2. Place the first spoke through the hole adjacent to the valve hole, followed by every subsequent fourth spoke hole in the rim.
3. Place the inboard spokes into the other side of the hub – viewed across the hub – place the first of these to the left of the spoke in the opposite flange. Now turn the hub so that the spokes are angled away from the valve hole.
4. Place the outboard spokes into the remaining holes in the drive side of the hub, then place the first of these under the crossing spoke and place it into the hole two places to the left serving that side of the hub.
5. Do the same for the remainder of the spokes, then turn the nipples until the spokes are held lightly under tension.
6. See page 122 (Wheel truing).

Spoke materials

Rustless spokes – these are galvanized steel and are cheaper than most stainless steel spokes. Their fatigue strength isn't as good as stainless spokes.

Stainless steel – these are found on more expensive bikes. They have a shiny appearance and don't corrode like so-called rustless spokes.

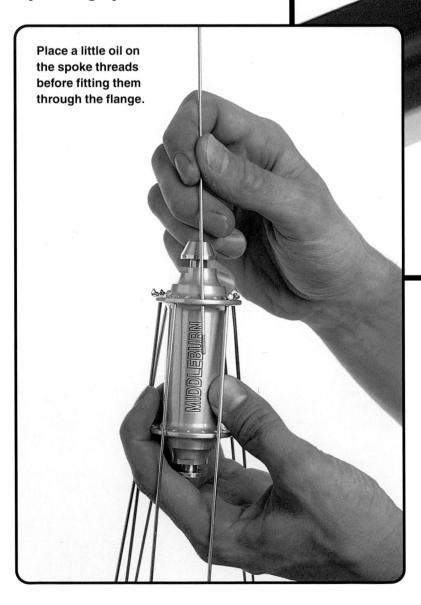

Place a little oil on the spoke threads before fitting them through the flange.

This rim has holes that are angled to enable the spokes to go to the left and right flanges. Be sure to put the spokes in the correct holes.

Spoke length

The spoke length is determined by the diameter of the flange, wheel size, number of spoke holes and the spoking pattern. Many shops have spoke-length charts for easy reference.

Spoking patterns

There are two ways to build a wheel. Crossing the spokes – where any one spoke is crossed by one, two or three others (termed three cross), and radial spoking – where the spokes radiate from the flange. The former provides an even load on the hub flange and an even pull of torque through the rim. The latter pulls directly on the hub flange, placing greater demands on the hub and rim, so the apparent weight saving of using shorter spokes is often lost by the need for a stronger hub and rim. The three cross pattern is the most reliable.

Half the job is done. With all the inboard spokes fitted, turn the hub anti-clockwise. Now fit the remaining spokes on the outboard side.

GEARS EXPLAINED

Bikes have more gears than cars for a good reason. You have limited horsepower on a bike – about 0.25 – and to make best use of that power your rev counter – the rate at which you pedal – needs to remain fairly constant.

You should be pedalling somewhere between 80 and 110rpm – at the low end for touring, and at the high end for racing. And you need to be able to keep that steady. On a flat road with no wind you could do this without changing gear. In real life situations you need a range of gears. Nowadays you've got them. In the past bikes had only one gear.

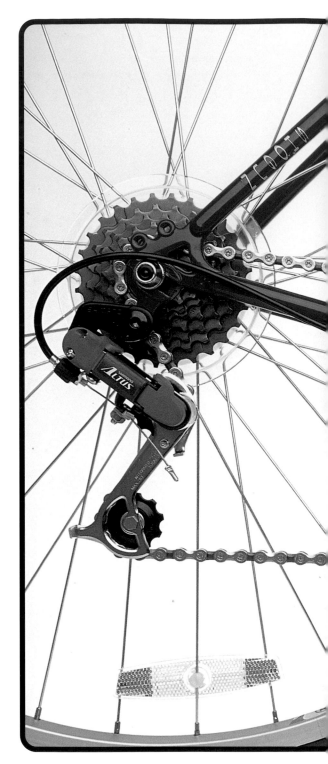

How gears work

In the days of the Penny Farthing, gearing was simple. The cranks were directly attached to the front wheel. Every time you turned the cranks through one revolution, the wheel turned through one revolution too. If your bike had a small wheel it wouldn't travel very far for each turn of the cranks. The bigger the wheel, the further the bike would travel for each crank rotation.

Since the rider sat above the wheel, the size of the wheel (and therefore the size of the gear) was restricted by the rider's inside leg measurement. If the wheel was too big, the rider couldn't reach the pedals!

The chain-driven safety bike was a vast improvement. In between the cranks and the drive wheel (now at the rear), were two cogs, the chainring and the sprocket. By varying the sizes of one or both of these cogs, you could alter the size of the gear.

Consider: if the chainring is twice as big as the sprocket, the wheel will revolve twice for each turn of the cranks. If it's four times as big, the wheel will revolve four times for each turn of the cranks. With the right chainring and sprocket, one turn of the cranks on a safety bike would enable you to travel much further – and, hills notwithstanding, much faster – than one turn of the cranks on a Penny Farthing.

Penny Farthings and most child's tricycles have the simplest form of gearing – direct drive, with the pedals attached to the wheel.

Derailleur gears

One early method of having a choice of gears was to have a differently sized sprocket on either side of the rear wheel. When you knew it was going to get hilly, you could swap the rear wheel around so that you could use the bigger sprocket, giving you a smaller gear.

Modern derailleurs are much better. You don't have to stop, take the wheel out and turn it round. You just shift a lever as you're riding along, and you have many more gears to

Shifting to a high gear lets you go further for each turn of the cranks, though it is correspondingly harder to pedal.

HUB GEARS

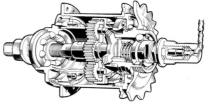

Hub gears operate using a system of cog wheels within the shell of the hub. The advantages are: the chain is always in line; the mechanics are protected from the weather; it's easy to use – you can't derail the chain; and you don't need to turn the cranks to change gear.

The disadvantage is that you are stuck with a narrower range of gears. But you can now buy 5 and 7-speed hubs, which means the spread of gears is getting better. You can also buy mixed hub gear and derailleur systems that do away with the need for a front changer, while 9-speed hub gears are on the way.

choose from. Six, seven or eight differently sized sprockets and two or three chainrings gives you a wide variety of gears to cope with all kinds of gradients and conditions.

You might have a 24-tooth chainring and a 32-tooth sprocket as your easiest gear, meaning that the wheel turns three-quarters round for each crank revolution, and a 48-tooth chainring and a 12-tooth sprocket as your hardest, meaning that the wheel turns four times per crank revolution.

DON'T USE ALL YOUR GEARS

When using derailleur gears, the chain should run as near as possible to straight along the line of its link plates. If it runs diagonally it is less efficient. This is why you should avoid using the smallest chainring at the same time as the smallest sprocket, and the biggest chainring with the biggest sprocket.

This is not a problem, as you'll see when you find out what all your different gear sizes are. You won't need to use the biggest chainring and the biggest sprocket; you can use a smaller chainring and a smaller sprocket to get approximately the same gear. There is a deliberate overlap – which means, incidentally, that there aren't 24 different gears on a 24-speed bike.

Using the small chainring with the biggest sprocket (main picture) is fine. But the large chainring and large sprocket combination (left) is duplicating a gear better obtained with a smaller chainring and smaller sprocket.

Measuring gears

Measuring gear size in terms of wheel rotations per crank revolution is cumbersome, and doesn't allow for comparisons between bikes with different wheel sizes. In Britain and America, gears are measured in inches.

This is a hangover from the days of Penny Farthings, when the size of the wheel was the size of the gear. A Penny Farthing with a 54-inch wheel had a 54-inch gear. The size of the gears for a modern bike is found by this formula:

$$\frac{\text{chainring size (number of teeth)}}{\text{sprocket size (number of teeth)}} \times \text{wheel diameter (inches)} = \text{gear size (inches)}$$

A modern bike with a 40-tooth chainring, a 20-tooth sprocket and a 27-inch wheel therefore has a gear of 54 inches. In a race with a 54-inch high Penny Farthing, with the cranks turning at the same speed, the two bikes would be neck and neck.

The gear size, then, is the effective diameter of the rear wheel. Though the measurement may seem arcane, it allows for accurate comparisons between gears, enabling you to choose a set-up that suits you best. We've compiled two tables showing common gear combinations overleaf.

The European method is to measure gear development. All this really does is throw pi (π) into the above equation, since it measures the distance travelled for one revolution of the cranks. In other words, it measures the effective wheel circumference.

With a single chainring, you don't need to worry about chainline unless you're changing your bottom bracket.

'Sprocket size (teeth)'

'Chainring size (teeth)'	11	12	13	14	15	16	17	18	19	20	21	22	23	24	25	26	27	28	29	30	31	32
20	47	43	40	37	35	33	31	29	27	26	25	24	23	22	21	20	19	19	18	17	17	16
21	50	46	42	39	36	34	32	30	29	27	26	25	24	23	22	21	20	20	19	18	18	17
22	52	48	44	41	38	36	34	32	30	29	27	26	25	24	23	22	21	20	20	19	18	18
23	54	50	46	43	40	37	35	33	31	30	28	27	26	25	24	23	22	21	21	20	19	19
24	57	52	48	45	42	39	37	35	33	31	30	28	27	26	25	24	23	22	22	21	20	20
25	59	54	50	46	43	41	38	36	34	33	31	30	28	27	26	25	24	23	22	22	21	20
26	61	56	52	48	45	42	40	38	36	34	32	31	29	28	27	26	25	24	23	23	22	21
27	64	59	54	50	47	44	41	39	37	35	33	32	31	29	28	27	26	25	24	23	23	22
28	66	61	56	53	49	46	43	40	38	36	35	33	32	30	29	28	27	26	25	24	24	23
29	69	63	58	54	50	47	44	42	40	38	36	34	33	31	30	29	28	27	26	25	24	24
30	71	65	60	56	52	49	46	43	41	39	37	36	34	33	31	30	29	28	27	26	25	24
31	73	67	62	58	54	50	47	45	42	40	38	37	35	34	32	31	30	29	28	27	26	25
32	76	69	64	59	56	52	49	46	44	42	40	38	36	35	33	32	31	30	29	28	27	26
33	78	72	66	61	57	54	51	48	45	43	41	39	37	36	34	33	32	31	30	29	28	27
34	80	74	68	63	59	56	52	49	47	44	42	40	38	37	35	34	33	32	31	30	29	28
35	83	76	70	65	61	57	54	51	48	46	43	41	40	38	36	35	34	33	31	30	29	28
36	85	78	72	67	62	59	55	52	49	47	45	43	41	39	37	36	35	33	32	31	30	29
37	87	80	74	69	64	60	57	53	51	48	46	44	42	40	39	37	36	34	33	32	31	30
38	90	82	76	71	66	62	58	55	52	49	47	45	43	41	40	38	37	35	34	33	32	31
39	92	85	78	72	68	63	60	56	53	51	48	46	44	42	41	39	38	36	35	34	33	32
40	95	87	80	74	69	65	61	58	55	52	50	47	45	43	42	40	39	37	36	35	34	33
41	97	89	82	76	71	67	63	59	56	53	51	49	46	44	43	41	40	38	37	36	34	33
42	99	91	84	78	73	68	64	61	58	55	52	50	48	46	44	42	40	39	38	36	35	34
43	102	93	86	80	75	70	66	62	59	56	53	51	49	47	45	43	41	40	39	37	36	35
44	104	95	88	82	76	72	67	64	60	57	55	52	50	48	46	44	42	41	39	38	37	36
45	106	98	90	84	78	73	69	65	62	59	56	53	51	49	47	45	43	42	40	39	38	37
46	109	100	92	85	80	75	70	66	63	60	57	54	52	50	48	46	44	43	41	40	39	37
47	111	102	94	87	82	76	72	68	64	61	58	56	53	51	49	47	45	44	42	41	39	38
48	113	104	96	89	83	78	73	69	66	62	59	57	54	52	50	48	46	45	43	42	40	39
49	116	106	98	91	85	80	75	71	67	64	61	58	55	53	51	49	47	46	44	43	41	40
50	118	108	100	93	87	81	77	72	68	65	62	59	57	54	52	50	48	46	45	43	42	41

(**NB.** Gears shown to nearest inch)

'Sprocket size (teeth)'

'Chainring size (teeth)'	11	12	13	14	15	16	17	18	19	20	21	22	23	24	25	26	27	28	29	30	31	32
24	59	54	50	46	43	41	38	36	34	32	31	30	28	27	26	25	24	23	22	22	21	20
25	61	56	52	48	45	42	40	38	36	34	32	31	29	28	27	26	25	24	23	23	22	21
26	64	59	54	50	47	44	41	39	37	35	33	32	31	29	28	27	26	25	24	23	23	22
27	66	61	56	52	49	46	43	41	38	36	35	33	32	30	29	28	27	26	25	24	24	23
28	69	63	58	54	50	47	45	42	40	38	36	34	33	32	30	29	28	27	26	25	24	24
29	71	65	60	56	52	49	46	44	41	39	37	36	34	33	31	30	29	28	27	26	25	25
30	74	68	62	58	54	51	48	45	43	41	39	37	35	34	32	31	30	29	28	27	26	25
31	76	70	64	60	56	52	49	47	44	42	40	38	36	35	34	32	31	30	29	28	27	26
32	79	72	67	62	58	54	51	48	46	43	41	39	38	36	35	33	32	31	30	29	28	27
33	81	74	69	64	59	56	52	50	47	45	42	41	39	37	36	34	33	32	31	30	29	28
34	83	77	71	66	61	57	54	51	48	46	44	42	40	38	37	35	34	33	32	31	30	29
35	86	79	73	68	63	59	56	53	50	47	45	43	41	39	38	36	35	34	33	32	31	30
36	88	81	75	69	65	61	57	54	52	49	46	44	42	41	39	37	36	35	34	32	31	30
37	91	83	77	71	67	62	59	56	53	50	48	45	43	42	40	38	37	36	35	33	32	31
38	93	86	79	73	68	64	60	57	54	51	49	47	45	43	41	40	38	37	35	34	33	32
39	96	88	81	75	70	66	62	59	55	53	50	48	46	44	42	41	39	38	36	35	34	33
40	98	90	83	77	72	68	64	60	57	54	51	49	47	45	43	42	40	39	37	36	35	34
41	101	92	85	79	74	69	65	62	58	55	53	50	48	46	44	43	41	40	38	37	36	35
42	103	95	87	81	76	71	67	63	60	57	54	52	49	47	45	44	42	41	39	38	37	35
43	106	97	89	83	77	73	68	65	61	58	55	53	51	48	46	45	43	42	40	39	38	36
44	108	99	91	85	79	74	70	66	63	60	57	54	52	50	48	46	44	42	41	40	38	37
45	110	101	94	87	81	76	72	68	64	61	58	55	53	51	49	47	45	43	42	41	39	38
46	113	104	96	89	83	78	73	69	65	62	59	57	54	52	50	48	46	44	43	41	40	39
47	115	106	98	91	85	79	75	71	67	64	60	58	55	53	51	49	47	45	44	42	41	40
48	118	108	100	93	86	81	76	72	68	65	62	59	56	54	52	50	48	46	45	43	42	41
49	120	110	102	95	88	83	78	74	70	66	63	60	58	55	53	51	49	47	46	44	43	41
50	123	113	104	96	90	84	79	75	71	68	64	61	59	56	54	52	50	48	47	45	44	42
51	125	115	106	98	92	86	81	77	73	69	66	63	60	57	55	53	51	49	48	46	44	43
52	128	117	108	100	94	88	83	78	74	70	67	64	61	59	56	54	52	50	48	47	45	44
53	130	119	110	102	95	89	84	80	75	72	68	65	62	60	57	55	53	51	49	48	46	45
54	133	122	112	104	97	91	86	81	77	73	69	66	63	61	58	65	54	52	50	49	47	46

(**NB.** Gears shown to nearest inch)

Below: This is the reason to avoid using the big ring and big sprocket (or little ring and little sprocket) – the chain runs diagonally, which is inefficient. It needs to run parallel to the line of its link plates.

THE FRONT DERAILLEUR

Grade of job: Easy to moderate
Tools: 5mm or 6mm Allen key, Pozidrive screwdriver

The front derailleur is made up of two plates called the cage plates. These plates shift sideways to derail the chain from chainring to chainring. The mech rarely gives problems if adjusted correctly. The most common fault is that the chain unships itself due to the mech being set too far from the chain rings.

High and low screw adjusters make it easy to get your front mech working properly. Be subtle with your adjustments though, a half turn can make the difference between a jammed chain and a smooth change.

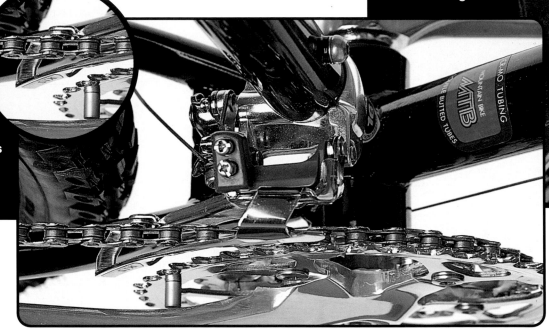

Keep the front mech and its moving parts clean and well lubed. The peg on the chainset (circled here) stops the chain from becoming entangled if it falls off.

Adjusting the front mech

1. Shift the gear control to select the smallest chain ring. Turn the cranks and look at the gap between the mech and the largest chainring. It should be between one and two millimetres. Loosen the fixing bolt and adjust for height but don't fully tighten yet.

2. Viewed from the top, the front mech must be at the correct angle to work properly. The rear part of the parallel plates (sometimes referred to as the cage plate), needs to be 2–3mm further towards your ankle than the front part of the cage. As you tighten the clamp bolt, the mech may twist; compensate for this by towing the cage plate outwards even more before tightening the bolt again.

3. Inspect the gear outer cable for cracks in the casing, especially at the ends. Replace any metal cable end caps that show signs of splitting. Inspect the gear inner cable for corrosion, especially where the cable is directly exposed.

4. Turn the barrel adjuster on the gear lever in a clockwise direction when viewed from the front, clamp the inner cable to the gear mech, but leave some cable slack in the case of Shimano STI, and no slack in the case of grip shifters.

If you have to remove a worn or damaged mech, don't split the chain – remove the screw at the back of the mech instead.

5. If you haven't got a workstand get someone to hold the rear wheel off the ground. Operate the gear lever, if it's slow to shift the chain onto the middle chainring turn the barrel adjuster at the end of the control cable anti-clockwise until if shifts cleanly. If it's slow to shift back down to the small chainring, adjust the inner gear limit screw by turning it anti-clockwise. Put the rear gear in the smallest sprocket and shift the chain onto the large chainring. If the chain rubs on the front gear mech turn the screw nearest the crank arm anti-clockwise until the chain is silent.

THE REAR DERAILLEUR

The rear derailleur draws the chain across the sprockets, according to the amount of pull actuated by the control lever. The distance between the jockey wheels on the mech determines its capacity to handle a ratio of gears – a long-arm mech will handle a wide ratio while a short-arm mech will handle a smaller ratio and provide a slightly faster, more direct shift than the long arm version. Although breakages are rare on a road bike, the long-arm mechs fitted to most MTBs are prone to breakage and, more commonly, wear caused by the action of mud and water on the moving parts.

If the gears become noisy – use the thumbwheel adjuster to tension the cable. Turn it anti-clockwise until the noise disappears.

Removal/replacement

1. Using the appropriate wrench, undo the cable anchor and pull the outer cable free from the gear mech. Undo the lower of the two jockey wheels, then remove the chain and the mech.

2. Fit the new mech, holding it as far back as possible. Turn the 5mm fitting bolt clockwise into the gear hanger. Don't use force; if you do you will cross the thread. Remove the lower jockey wheel bolt on the new mech, then loosen the upper one. Thread the chain over and under the lower wheel, then tighten both jockey wheel bolts.

3. Inspect the cables for broken strands then thread the inner cable through the mech barrel adjuster and clamp it, using a 5mm Allen key or 8mm wrench.

4. Put the chain on the smallest chain ring then, using your hands, move the rear mech across to the largest rear sprocket. If the chain runs into the spokes turn the screw marked 'L' clockwise until it doesn't. Let go of the mech and observe the way it shifts to the smallest sprocket. Turn the screw marked 'H' clockwise if the mech moves too far and jams the chain into the frame. Move the same screw anti clockwise if the chain rests on the second smallest sprocket.

Short arm mechs (top) provide fast direct shifting, but they are only suitable for smaller gear ratios. Long arm mechs (bottom) are commonly found on MTBs and tourers.

The two screws positioned on the back of the rear mech (right) limit the amount that the mech moves and should only require adjustments if you change the cogs.

TIPS

> In the event of a crash, a spoke protector (a round disc that fits behind the cassette), will prevent the mech from being caught and possibly broken by the spokes of your rear wheel.

> If excessive wear is evident in the jockey wheels replacements can be obtained.

> If you are replacing a long-arm mech with a short one, don't forget to add some extra links to your chain. Make sure the chain works all right on the largest chain wheel and the largest sprocket before you hit the road or trail.

With the lower jockey wheel removed the mech is now separated from the chain. Worn jockey wheels can be replaced in this way, but remember to tighten the bolts firmly.

GEAR CABLES AND SHIFTERS

The beginner's guide to gear levers

If you're using them for the first time, gears can be a daunting prospect. But don't panic; modern shifters have user friendly click stops. This system, called indexing, is common to a number of different gear changers.

Grip shift

Grip shift is very popular with beginners. The rider rotates the grip to change gear. Moving the grip towards you makes it easier to pedal up a hill; twisting the grip away, provides a gear that's harder to push and is ideal for the flat or descents.

Shimano STI (MTB)

Strong, reliable and very popular. The STI gear control is positioned beneath the handlebar. Each changer has two levers. The bottom lever provides a slower pedalling rate for downhill, while pressing the top lever makes it easier to climb gradients.

Shimano STI (road)/Campagnolo Ergo

Expensive shifters for road-race bikes. The mechanics of the two systems are different, but the aim is the same – convenient gear changing. With both systems, the shifters form part of the brake lever, with Shimano favouring a lever set-up over the Campag button design.

Thumb shifters

Old system but very reliable and simple to maintain. Using the thumb and forefinger, pushing the lever away with your thumb gives you a higher gear. Drawing the lever back towards you makes it easy to climb hills.

WORKSHOP NOTES

> You'll need a no 1 pozidriver. Allen keys are available from all good tool shops.

> Ask for genuine grip shift gear inner cables; they have a smooth exterior which works best.

> Only use solvents recommended by the manufacturer. Special attention should be taken when working on high end grip shifters as they are prone to breakage after contact with some chemicals.

Service your grip shift

If there's one shifter that needs regular looking after it's the grip shift. Follow these tips and it'll last a lot longer.

1. Remove the grips using a long screwdriver and either washing up liquid or a spray lube, coat the screwdriver blade liberally with the lubricant and work it round between the grip and handlebar before yanking the grips.
2. Remove the brake levers and shifters using the correct size Allen keys then remove the mech retaining plate. This is held by a screw. Remove the cable from the housing.
3. Clean all parts using diluted washing up liquid or special grip shift solvent and a toothbrush, paying particular attention to the indents around the barrel.
4. Liberally coat all mating surfaces with Vaseline or special lube. Examine the gear inner cable for broken strands then thread it through the hole in the housing.
5. Offer up the barrel to the housing, loop the cable once round the barrel and through the adjuster. Gently push the grip shifter barrel into the housing and over the indent spring. You may have to push the cable home with a knife blade or blunt screwdriver before the barrel will press home. Attach the mech retaining plate and tighten the cross-headed screw then check that all the clicks are there.
6. Place the separating washer between the grip shift and the handlebar grip then spray the handlebar and inside of the grip with hairspray or a 'dry' lube.
7. Position the brake levers and tighten the clamp bolts. Set the grip shifters so there's at least 4mm between the barrel adjuster and the bottom of the brake lever. Tighten the Allen screw just enough to prevent movement.
8. Slide the outer cable section onto the inner cable and fix the inner cables to the front and rear mech clamps. Check and adjust the gears to index correctly using the adjuster barrel on the grip shift and the rear mech.

Make sure cables are routed neatly to prevent wear and friction.

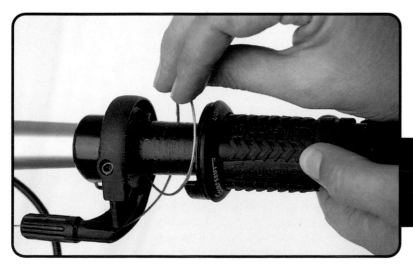

Before removing the old cable, make a note as to how it's routed – some grip shifts require the cable to be looped around the barrel of the unit.

THE BOTTOM BRACKET

Grade of job: Difficult.
Tools: 8mm Allen key or 14mm socket wrench, Adjustable spanner, Crank extractor,
Bottom bracket removal tool.

It's not just because it has the largest bearings on the bike that the bottom bracket is called 'the big end of the bicycle'. The bottom bracket carries the force of your efforts through the cranks and chain to the rear wheel.

Most bikes now use a one-piece bottom bracket unit that requires no adjustment of the bearings after fitting. Older style bikes and some budget bikes still use cup and axle bottom brackets. They can be identified by the locking ring on the left-hand side and a fixed cup on the right-hand side.

Servicing a cup and axle bottom bracket

1. Remove the cranks and turn the axle. If it feels at all rough or can be spun without resistance from the grease, it warrants further investigation.
2. Using a 'C spanner', turn the lock ring anti-clockwise followed by the left-hand bearing cup. Lift the axle and bearings from the frame then remove the fixed cup using a fixed cup spanner.
3. Clean and inspect the bearing lands for pitting, and more especially the axle bearing lands. If all is well, apply grease to the cups and fit new replacement bearings (usually ¼in). If in doubt, take the old bearings to your local shop for identification.
4. Turning it anti-clockwise, fit and tighten the fixed cup, then place the axle through the frame being careful not to dislodge any bearings. Screw the adjustable cup into the frame in a clockwise direction, followed by the lock ring.
5. Holding the adjustable cup with a pin spanner, tighten the lock ring very firmly.

Measure the overall distance of the bottom bracket to establish the axle length you require.

6. If you can feel resistance when turning the axle, slacken off the lock ring and turn the adjustable cup very slightly anti-clockwise. Now tighten the lock ring again. If all is well, fit the right-hand crank and tighten using a torque wrench (22 ft/lb). Grasp the crank arm, if play is evident, loosen the lock ring and turn the adjustable cup very slightly clockwise. Tighten the lock ring, and fit the left-hand crank.

Tips for fitting a cartridge bottom bracket

1. If you're removing a Shimano cartridge unit, remove the shoulderless cup first, followed by the other side. The cups unscrew in the same manner as the unit described above.
2. Don't put grease on the axle tapers; it makes the cranks go on further than is good for them.
3. If the cranks regularly come loose, it's likely that the tapers are damaged. Inspect them, if a taper is swaged at the edges, replace it.
4. Bottom bracket cups on Italian frames loosen in an anti-clockwise direction.
5. Before you ask your cycle shop for a replacement, measure the overall width of the old bottom bracket unit and the width of the bottom bracket shell on your bike; the latter for road and MTBs is usually 68mm though some use a 72mm shell.

Main picture (below) A Shimano bottom bracket tool is used to remove the bottom bracket. If one cup is plastic, remove it after first loosening the other side.

To get maximum leverage from an adjustable spanner, hold the tool at its end.

Left: Use a 5mm Allen key to fit and remove the chainring bolts. The chainrings are retained by the 'Spider', in this case coloured red.

Replacement chainrings should use the correct bolt fixing.

THE CHAINSET

Grade of job: Moderate.
Tools: 5mm and 8mm Allen keys,
Crank extractor, 14mm or 15mm socket wrench, Shimano chainring nut tool.

The chainset fits onto a taper at each end of the bottom bracket axle. It's pressed onto the taper by tightening a bolt – usually an 8mm Allen key or a 14mm hex headed bolt. Because it is forced onto the taper a maximum torque setting of around 22 ft/lb should be adhered to. A torque wrench can be obtained for under £20 though you'll need a socket set and an Allen key adaptor socket.

Changing the chainrings

Shimano and Sugino chainrings have a worn appearance even before they've been used. It's those bent and cutaway teeth that help the chain to ramp the gears smoothly. But problems will occur if more teeth get bent or broken. Replacing chainrings is pretty straightforward, though some fettling may be required with the American chainsets. It helps to measure the distance between your original chainrings, as in extreme cases you may have to add spacers to achieve the same set-up as you had before.

1. Clean the whole drivetrain using degreaser. Check whether the rings need replacment. A bent tooth is easy to see and can be straightened using an adjustable spanner.
2. Measure the distance across the bolt fixing points – older style chainsets use outer chainrings which measure 110mm across the fixing bolts. The other size typically found on low pro chainsets is 94mm.
3. Turn the 5mm Allen headed fitting bolts anti-clockwise to loosen them, then remove the crank arm using a crank extractor. Remove the worn rings from the chainset spider. Leave the chainset on the axle if you're only changing the outer chain ring.
4. Place the new chainrings over the crank

The backs of the chainring retaining nuts should be held using a special Shimano tool – as shown here.

The black chainring is an example of extreme tooth wear, while the lower is a new replacment chainring.

spider. If you're changing the middle ring fit it so the nut is flush. Oil the nut threads. Holding the back of the nuts with your fingers, turn the Allen bolts clockwise until finger tight. Now use the special Shimano chainring nut tool and a 5mm Allen key to fully tighten the bolts.

5. Fit and tighten the crank onto the axle using a torque wrench.

6. Set the front mech high and low gear limits.

7. Go ride the bike. If the chain hesitates or sucks between the chainrings, measure the distance between the chainrings again. Fit spacers behind the middle chainring if the chain drops or slips between the middle and inner chainrings.

TIPS

> Remember to adjust the height of the mech if you're fitting a chainring with more teeth.

> Compact drive inner chainrings are 56mm across the fixing holes.

> Always use the special Shimano tool for holding aluminium chainring fixing nuts.

> If fitted, align the peg on the outer chainring as close to the crank arm as possible, preferably behind it.

> Unless you have a particular problem with aluminium chainring bolts, avoid using locking agent on the threads – it makes them very difficult to remove later.

> It's less crucial to replace worn chain rings than it is to replace a worn cassette.

[A chainring nut holding tool is available from Madison Cycles, UK.]

CASSETTES

Grade of job: Moderate.
Tools: Chain rivet tool, Chain whip, Cassette lockring tool, Chain wear gauge.

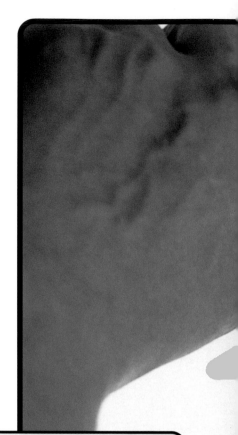

When new, the chain's rollers sit comfortably on the sprocket teeth and spread the load evenly. As the chain wears, the load is concentrated in certain areas, which causes further deterioration. If you let this go on too long the sprockets become hooked. And, if you try to put a new chain onto hooked sprockets it will jump. The wear process can be slowed down by replacing your chain at regular intervals.

You may find that your chain has worn too far for a new chain to be compatible with your cassette. The symptom is a skipping chain, and a replacement cassette or freewheel is the only answer.

Changing a cassette

1. Clean the chain and the spaces between the sprockets with degreaser. Leave the cleaner for several minutes to melt the grime, then wash it off with a washing-up brush. If you need to use a hose, wrap a rag behind the cassette to prevent any moisture getting into the cassette body and use a moisture dispersant after washing.

2. Check the sprockets for worn teeth. The largest sprocket is usually the first to take on a hooked appearance.

3. To remove a cassette cluster, place a chain whip on the middle sprocket and put the extractor tool into the end of the cassette – use a large spanner for extra leverage. Bear down on the spanner and chain whip to release the lockring that holds the cassette on.

4. Place the new cassette over the cassette body, screw on the lockring and tighten using the extractor tool.

5. Using the old chain as a guide, split the new chain at the same rivet and thread it through the jockey wheels. Join the chain and free off the stiff link using the upper part of the chain tool to separate the links.

6. Check the gears before setting off.

The cassette sprockets on the left are extremely worn and will cause erratic gear shifting in muddy conditions. The right is a new example.

JARGON BUSTER

JOCKEY WHEELS: These are the guide wheels that make up the lower part of a rear gear mech.

CASSETTE BODY: This is the part that the cassette sprockets fit onto.

Left: Get a firm grip on the tools as the cassette lock-ring is usually a very firm fit on the sprocket cluster.

Above: Use a hacksaw blade to remove muck that has acumulated between the cassette sprockets.

Some sprocket clusters (in this case Campagnolo) are loose and must be aligned using the markings on the sprockets.

TIPS

> Don't fit a new cassette on its own; a used chain will probably slip.

> Campagnolo cassette sprockets are supplied loose. Align them on the cassette body correctly using the instructions supplied with the cassette.

> There are several brands of weight saving cassettes available, such as Marchisio and Goldtech.

> It's possible to use a Shimano cassette with a Campagnolo gear train or vice versa. You can do this by fitting different spacers between the cassette sprockets. Contact Ison Distribution

THE CHAIN

Grade of job: Easy.
Tools: Chain rivet extractor, Washing up brush, Park Chain Checker or ruler, Biodegradable solvent

The chain has the unenviable task of transmitting your efforts through to the rear wheel, so it's commonly the first component to wear out. Chains are made up of rollers, plates and pins and are available in different widths to account for the distance between the rear cogs. There is a chain for five, six, seven and eight speed systems. The last is particularly narrow.

A chain wear gauge is an economical way of checking the wear on a chain. It will enable you to replace your chain before it causes your sprockets to become hooked.

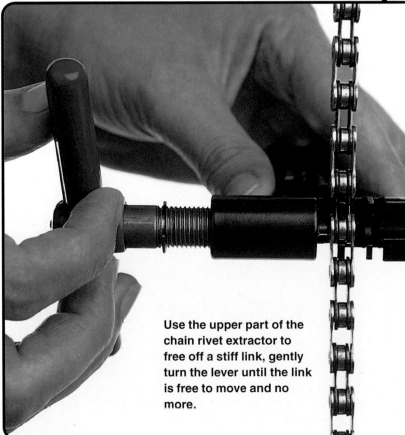

Use the upper part of the chain rivet extractor to free off a stiff link, gently turn the lever until the link is free to move and no more.

How to measure chain wear

1. Using a biodegradable solvent, clean the chain thoroughly then dry.
2. Using a ruler, measure from the centre of any pin to the centre of the pin approximately 12 inches away. If the pin is at less than 12 $\frac{1}{16}$in, the chain is fine, if it's between 12 $\frac{1}{16}$in and 12 $\frac{1}{8}$in consider replacing it, and if it's at 12 $\frac{1}{8}$in or more replace it immediately. Specially designed chain wear checkers are available if you don't like the ruler technique.
3. If you have to remove a non-Shimano

A chain cleaner saves time and confines the mess created as the links are cleaned.

TIPS

> If you've got a 16 or a 24-speed transmission, be sure to replace a worn chain with the correct 8-speed compatible version.

> Current Sachs chains (stamped with the letters PG) are compatible with all Shimano cassettes.

> Shimano's 1995 IG chains, prefixed IG30 and IG50, aren't compatible with HG cassettes, so ask before buying a discounted chain by mail order.

chain, use a chain tool but don't push the pin all the way through. Push it just enough to separate the chain. Don't drive out the black pin found on Shimano chains.

4. To rejoin the chain use a chain tool to press the pin through. In the case of a Shimano chain, fit a special black pin through the ends and press it home using the extractor.

5. The link you have joined will be stiff. To cure this, use the upper part of the chain tool or simply flex the chain until the link is free to move. Check that the pin protrudes equally from either side of the chain.

Lubing the chain

It's vital to keep the chain well oiled for it to work smoothly. You can lubricate your chain with a number of different types of lube. A dry lube – so called as it contains Teflon which is a tenacious and non-sticky lubricant – foams out of the spray can and penetrates the links of the chain. It is ideal for dry, dusty conditions.

Wet lubes, such as mineral and synthetic oils, don't need reapplying as often as dry lubes in wet, gritty conditions. However, they attract dirt particles so the chain requires frequent cleaning.

HUB GEARS

Hub gears are sealed from the elements and require little more maintenance than the occasional drop of oil – some don't even have an oil cap and are sealed for life, requiring no maintenance.

The gear ratios are effected by a cable-operated push rod which brings different groups of internal cogs into mesh. The range, of course, isn't as big as a derailleur system because they can only be used with a single chainwheel. The range of gears for Shimano's popular seven-speed hub is 33in–79in when fitted to a hybrid bike with 700/35 wheels. This provides a useful range for leisure riding and light touring but is insufficient for those who intend to carry heavy loads.

Sachs, Sturmey Archer and Shimano all produce hub gears, the last of which is available with a hub brake.

To adjust a Sturmey Archer hub gear all you have to do is turn the toggle chain adjuster.

Thumbshifters are used to operate most hub gears. They are easy to maintain and give positive gear changes.

Fitting a hub gear and brake system

Grade of job: Easy.
Tools: 15mm spanner, 10mm spanner (x 2), 3mm Allen key.

The Shimano Nexus hub gear is available in four and seven-speed versions and can be fitted to any bike which uses a derailleur gear. These instructions cover the four-speed version.

> ### TIP
>
> > If you find the chain constantly becomes loose, it's likely that the hub is slipping in the dropouts. Complement the existing gripper nut with a second one, this time behind the dropout.

1. The system is supplied partially assembled – a special pin keeps the mechanism in alignment while the control cable is being fitted. With the handlebar control in first gear, place the inner cable through the anchor point and tighten it with a 3mm Allen key. The hub and the actuating ring are in alignment when the two yellow triangles line up. Now fit the circlip supplied with the kit and remove the nail from the bayonet ring.
2. Fit the rear wheel into the frame. Pull it back in the frame until there's no slack in the chain, check there are no tight spots by back pedalling. Fit the brake plate ring around the chain stay and tighten the bolt and special nut – usually a 10mm bolt and nut.
3. Run the control cable back along the frame and route to carefully avoid the chain rings – use the special clamps supplied with the kit or cable ties available from an electrical wholesaler.
4. Fine tune the gear by placing the handlebar control in fourth gear, then align the red pips on the top part of the bayonet ring, and turn the adjuster to the appropriate position.

Maintaining a three-speed hub gear

Grade of job: Moderate.
Tools: 15mm spanner for the tracknuts, 10mm spanners (x 2), Cable cutters.

1. Using the flip cap filler on the hub body, insert about 10 drops of oil into the hub, then close the cap.
2. Slipping gears can be rectified by adjusting the chain through the hole in the locknut. Position the handlebar trigger control in second gear. The end of the linked part of the toggle chain should be flush with the end of the axle.
3. If there's insufficient adjustment to pull the toggle to the required position, loosen the cable stop and move it forwards by about one centimetre.

Removal and replacement of a Sachs seven-speed wheel.

Grade of job: Easy to moderate.
Tools: 15mm wrench.

The Sachs hub is particularly user-friendly when you have to remove the rear wheel.

1. Go to the long plastic actuator unit by the right-hand side of the rear axle, undo the gnurled screw on the top of the actuator, then lift the actuator away from the axle. Remove the grey plastic widget followed by the thin actuator rod and put them in a safe place.
2. Undo the track nuts and tab washers, then lift the wheel from the bike.
3. Fitting is the reverse of removal but make sure that the cut-out on the grey plastic widget is pointing forwards before you replace the actuator unit. You may have to manipulate the gears to get it to seat but when it does you will hear a firm click. Don't forget to tighten the gnurled screw on the top.

The Sachs gear cable actuator unit (above) is a neat looking device.

Combined gear and brake lever units such as the Campagnolo Ergopower (shown here) are secured using a 5mm Allen key.

CALIPER BRAKES

Caliper brakes, as used on most drop handlebar bikes, remained unchanged until dual pivot brakes were introduced by Shimano in the late 1980s.

A caliper brake has two U-shaped arms which pivot and are drawn together by the action of a cable. Unlike cantilever brakes, the leverage ratio of a caliper brake is not adjustable (ie they can't be tuned to give more or less bite). This is not a problem for road race bikes but tourists may need to adjust their brakes when carrying heavy panniers. Calipers also collect mud, so they're unsuitable for mountain bikes. All but the cheapest calipers have maintenance-free pivot bushes and consequently need little maintenance at all.

Fitting a caliper brake

Grade of job: Easy.
Tools: 5mm Allen key, adjustable spanner and cone spanner.

Fitting and adjusting a caliper brake is simple and requires few tools.

1. Using a 5mm Allen key, position the caliper on the frame. It's important to ensure there's at least 5mm of thread for the Allen nut to bite onto. Remove a spacer washer if necessary.
2. Fit the cable and centre the brake blocks. You can toe some brake blocks inwards to prevent squeaking (caused by the vibration of the brake block against the rim). If you can't achieve this on your brakes, use an adjustable spanner to manipulate the caliper arms until there's 1mm of tow in on the leading edge of the brake block.
3. Adjust the brake using a cone spanner.

Brake blocks can be 'toed-in' by manipulating the caliper arm with an adjustable spanner.

If it's not possible to centre the brakes using a cone spanner use an Allen key instead

Adjusting brakes

It's common for brakes to rub on one side of the rim. This is due to the action of the spring. Equalize the spring to avoid this situation. Place the end of an appropriate cone spanner on the centre of the brake and turn it until the brake blocks are positioned equidistantly from the rim when you squeeze the brake lever.

Fitting brake levers

Grade of job: Moderate.
Tools: Allen keys and ruler.

Fitting cables, which run beneath handlebar tape, is more tricky.

1. Loosen the Allen headed bolt inside the brake lever and slide the lever into position on the handlebars. Use a ruler to level the levers, then tighten the clamp bolts with an Allen key.
2. Place a cable end cap over the piece of outer cable you are going to use then put it through the back of the lever. Use electrician's tape at 3 inch intervals to secure the cable to the handlebars.
3. Untape the cable adjacent to the brake lever and pull the cable out from the back of the lever, then pass the inner cable through the brake lever blade and into the back of the lever. Daylight through the cable should guide your route.
4. Turn the cable adjuster (where fitted) on the caliper so that the cable stop is as close to the clamp as possible. Oil the inner cable before passing it through the outer cable. Thread it through the cable clamp on the caliper then squeeze the handlebar lever several times to seat the cable.
5. Pull the cable through the clamp so that there's about 2–3cm of movement at the lever before the brakes bite.
6. Handlebar tape usually comes with two short pieces of tape – place these behind the brake levers, around the clamps. Wind the finishing tape around the bars, working from the ends of the handlebar. When fitting Ergopower levers be careful that the tape doesn't interfere with the mechanism.

> **Finishing touches...use a cable end cap to prevent the brake cable from fraying.**

CANTILEVER BRAKES

Grade of job: Easy to moderate
Tools: 5mm and 1.5mm (for Shimano), Allen keys,
8, 9 and 10mm spanners, Cable cutters, Cone spanners (for Dia Compe cantilevers)

The brakes are the most important part of your bike, particularly if you ride off-road on a regular basis. Regular checks and replacement of worn parts should ensure you have safe brakes. The cantilever brake is simple, easy to maintain and is favoured by mountain bikers. Cantilevers also weigh less than other types of braking system.

Fitting a cantilever

1. Remove the cantilevers from their bosses and clean the mating surfaces. Grease the bosses before fitting them back on. If a spring is visible, place it through the middle of the three holes adjacent to the boss. Once tightened the cantilevers should turn freely. Position the brake blocks with the arrows (where present) pointing forwards and square to the rim then hand-tighten the securing nut.

2. Turn the brake lever adjuster fully clockwise then inspect the brake inner cable. If it's damaged, make sure you grease the new inner cable before threading it through the outer section – use the lined variety if you're replacing a damaged outer cable and don't forget to fit metal end caps.

3. Slide the inner cable through the straddle clamp and fit the straddle wire through the

anchor bolt on the cantilever. The straddle wire makes up a triangle – the squatter the triangle the stronger the braking power, with a taller triangle giving a softer bite. For maximum braking power, position the straddle clamp 1½in to 2in from the rear tyre and the brake blocks as far forward in the clamps as possible.

4. Shimano straddle wires have a button-shaped junction that's marked for easy cable alignment. Pull the brake inner cable through until it aligns with the line on the button-shaped junction then firmly tighten the cantilever cable clamp bolt.

5. Position the brake blocks approximately 2mm from the braking surface then toe-in the leading edge of the block. Use paper folded over three times to get the gap at the trailing edge of the block. Check there's at least 2mm of clearance between the blocks and the sidewall of the tyre when fully inflated, then tighten the brake block clamp bolt.

5. Pull the brake lever back hard to seat and stretch the cable. Loosen and pull the cable through the anchor bolt if the brake lever comes back further than half way.

7. If a block drags on the rim, adjust the spring tension. Older style Shimano cantilevers use a tiny cross headed or grub screw; turn it clockwise to reduce drag on that arm, turn anti-clockwise if it's dragging on the other side. To adjust Dia Compe cantilevers very slightly, loosen the main 5mm Allen bolt then, using a cone spanner, turn the spanner away from the bike to increase tension. Finally, tighten the 5mm Allen bolt whilst holding the cone spanner in the same position.

Straddle cables should be at 90 degrees to the cantilever arms, or as in this case aligned with the mark on the button-shaped junction.

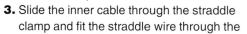

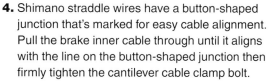

WORKSHOP NOTES

> If you're fitting new cantilevers make sure all the bits are there and read the instructions carefully.
> Sub-16in frames can have heel clearance problems. If you set-up the cantilevers for maximum leverage replace the Shimano unit straddle for a conventional straddle clamp.

> If the frame has just been re-finished make sure there's no paint on the cantilever boss. If there is, carefully remove with emery cloth and clean the boss thread with a 6mm finishing tap.

Above: Hold the brake block in place with an Allen key and secure it with a 10mm ring spanner.

Right: Before tightening a brake block place some paper beneath the rear of the block to help toe it in.

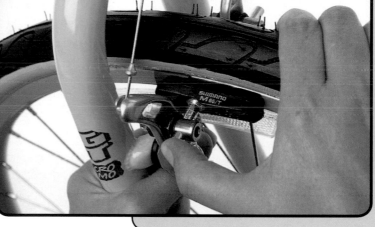

Sorting your cantilevers

> If the brake lever comes back more than half the available travel, the cable has stretched. Loosening the anchor bolt on the cantilever arm (it's usually a 5mm Allen bolt or 8mm nut), draw the control cable through the anchor point with pliers. Leave about 2mm of space between the brake blocks and the rims on either side. Now tighten the anchor bolt fully.

> If the brake block rubs on one side but releases itself when you turn the

wheel again – you have a wear lip on the brake block. This is common after a wet ride or after prolonged use and can be removed with a sharp knife, a flat file or sandpaper.

> If your brake blocks are flat yet still rub on the rim go to point 7 on page 156. The older style Shimano cantilevers mentioned there are adjusted using a 2mm Allen key which can be obtained from most DIY and hardware stores.

Check blocks for wear. Clear stones with a knife.

POWER BRAKES

Powerful stopping systems like disc brakes and V-brakes are popular for downhill racing and downhill speed record attempts. Disc brakes, in particular, need very little maintenance and provide exceptional outright stopping power.

Turn the screw clockwise if the brakes are dragging on this side.

Magura brakes use a hydraulic line that's attached to the brake lever with an olive-shaped seal (see below).

The V-brake

This is the natural progression from the cantilever. It uses one continuous cable – rather than a cable and straddle wire – to draw the brake arms together, so the compression on the brake arms is more direct than with a cantilever.

Fitting a V-brake

Grade of job: Moderate.
Tools: 5mm Allen key, Pozidrive or flat bladed screwdriver, Grease.

1. Make sure the kit is complete and that the package has not been disturbed. The instructions list the parts required – Shimano's official fitting instructions are excellent, so don't throw them away!
2. Fit the special bolt and be sure to locate the washer properly. Observe the instructions written on the brake blocks.
3. Put the concertina seal over the cable that lies between the V-brake arms and anchor the cable using a 5mm Allen key.
4. Change the spacer washers around if the concertina seal is compressed or there's less than 39mm between the arms.
5. Hold the brake blocks against the rim and fully tighten the 6mm Allen bolt. Pull the cable through the anchor clamp, leaving a gap of 1mm between the brake blocks and each side of the rim.
6. Squeeze the lever to seat the cable. If one arm drags on the rim, turn the adjustment screw on that arm clockwise until there's equal clearance.

Above: Hub brakes require a mounting point. They can be attached by either a P-shaped clip or, as in this case, a braze-on.

Left: Disc brakes crop up on all sorts of bikes. This example is a set up for a three wheeled recumbent.

The disc brake

Cable-operated disc brakes are suited to the high loads associated with tandem bicycles and MTB downhill racing. Brakes such as the Hope disc are operated by a worm drive which presses the disc pads against the disc.

Nexus brake

The Shimano Nexus brake is similar in principal to a hub brake but uses iron plates which act on the drum in place of brake shoes.

The U brake

These were popular in the mid-1980s and were commonly fitted to the rear of MTBs. As their name suggests, they are in the shape of a U. Performance is comparable to the best cantilever brakes and mud clearance using this design was excellent, but manufacturers dropped them in favour of the lighter weight cantilever brake.

The hub brake

Hub brakes are used mainly on utility bicycles and tandems where ultimate braking counts above the low weight of a cantilever or disc systems. A pair of brake shoes inside the drum are pressed against the inside surface of the drum by a cam.

Adjusting a cable on a hub brake system

If the brake lever begins to pull further toward the handlebar rather than at the beginning of its travel there is probably wear in the brake blocks or brake shoes. To adjust the brake, follow the three easy steps below.

Adjusting a hub brake

Grade of job: Easy.
Tools: Appropriate spanner for the adjustable barrel nipple (where fitted).

1. Turn the lockring on the gnurled adjuster on the end of the brake lever anti-clockwise. Then turn the small adjuster ring anti-clockwise until there's about 2cm of freeplay in the lever before it bites.
2. If you've turned the adjuster beyond the thread, turn it back in completely and loosen the cable clamp down by the cantilever or the actuating arm of the drum brake. Then pull a little cable through using pliers – drum brakes mostly use an adjustable barrel nipple.
3. Tighten the cable clamp, then spin the wheel to check the brakes don't bind. If they do, slacken the cable clamp bolt until you achieve the 2cm of lever travel before the brake bites. Firmly tighten the cable clamp bolt.

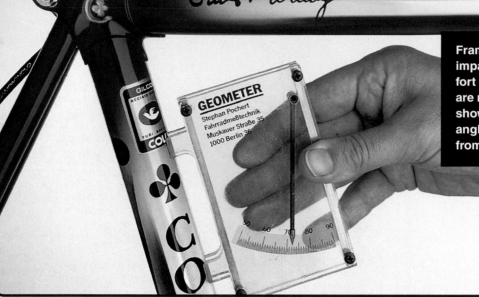

Frame geometry has a major impact on the handling and comfort of your bike. Frame angles are measured with the device shown left and represent the angle the seat tube deviates from the vertical.

BIKE FRAMES

Geometry and design

The majority of bicycle frames use the double triangle. This design positions the saddle, wheels and handlebars in a way that's convenient for the rider. Frame angles and tube lengths determine how the bike handles. The design must give sufficient ground clearance for cornering, and must avoid 'overlap' – the rider's feet brushing the front wheel. At the turn of the century, all bikes had shallow, angular frames which gave stability on poor road surfaces; similarly, modern MTBs use shallow frame angles for stability over rough ground. As road surfaces have improved – and in the case of MTBs, as suspension forks were available – more upright frame angles have been used. These frames give a responsive aspect to steering which is particularly useful for the swift changes of direction needed for sprint racing. Oval racing track bikes, with frame angles of 75 degrees from the vertical, are an extreme example of the trend towards steeper frame angles.

Is your frame the correct size?

The further you ride the more you will become aware of the aches and pains which indicate that you need to adjust your bike to improve the quality of your cycling. If your bike is the right size (see page 22) you will be able to adjust it without the need for an outrageously long or short stem. However, if you have already committed yourself to a bike that isn't the right size, changing the handlebars, stem or seatpost may ease your plight.

Get the right bike

It's easy to get the right bike the first time. A reputable bike shop will provide you with an informed opinion which could save you hundreds of pounds in the long run. Measuring up for a tourer or a road race bike is different to measuring up for an MTB. The MTB frame is

Even mass-produced bikes come in a wide range of sizes. Make sure you get the right size – don't just take the bike your shop has in stock.

Unicrown forks, as found on most MTBs. They are lightweight, reliable and extremely strong. These forks are also ideally suited for the fitting of bosses for cantilever brakes. Some road bikes are now fitted with unicrown forks.

smaller for manoeuvrability and has a lower top tube which gives crutch clearance – this avoids nasty injuries when riders are unseated suddenly. Straddle the top tube and lift the handlebar; 2–3 inches of lift is the minimum requirement.

For touring bikes, measure your inside leg and multiply by 0.68. This figure should be close to that measured from the centre of the bottom bracket to the centre of the seat tube. Massed start riders require a more aerodynamic position so subtract 2cm from this figure for road bikes.

Saddle setback

Using a plumb bob (a weight on the end of a piece of thread) and a ruler, align the string with the bottom bracket bolt and measure the distance from where the string crosses the top tube to the tip of the saddle. Using the chart below, adjust the saddle to the appropriate figure.

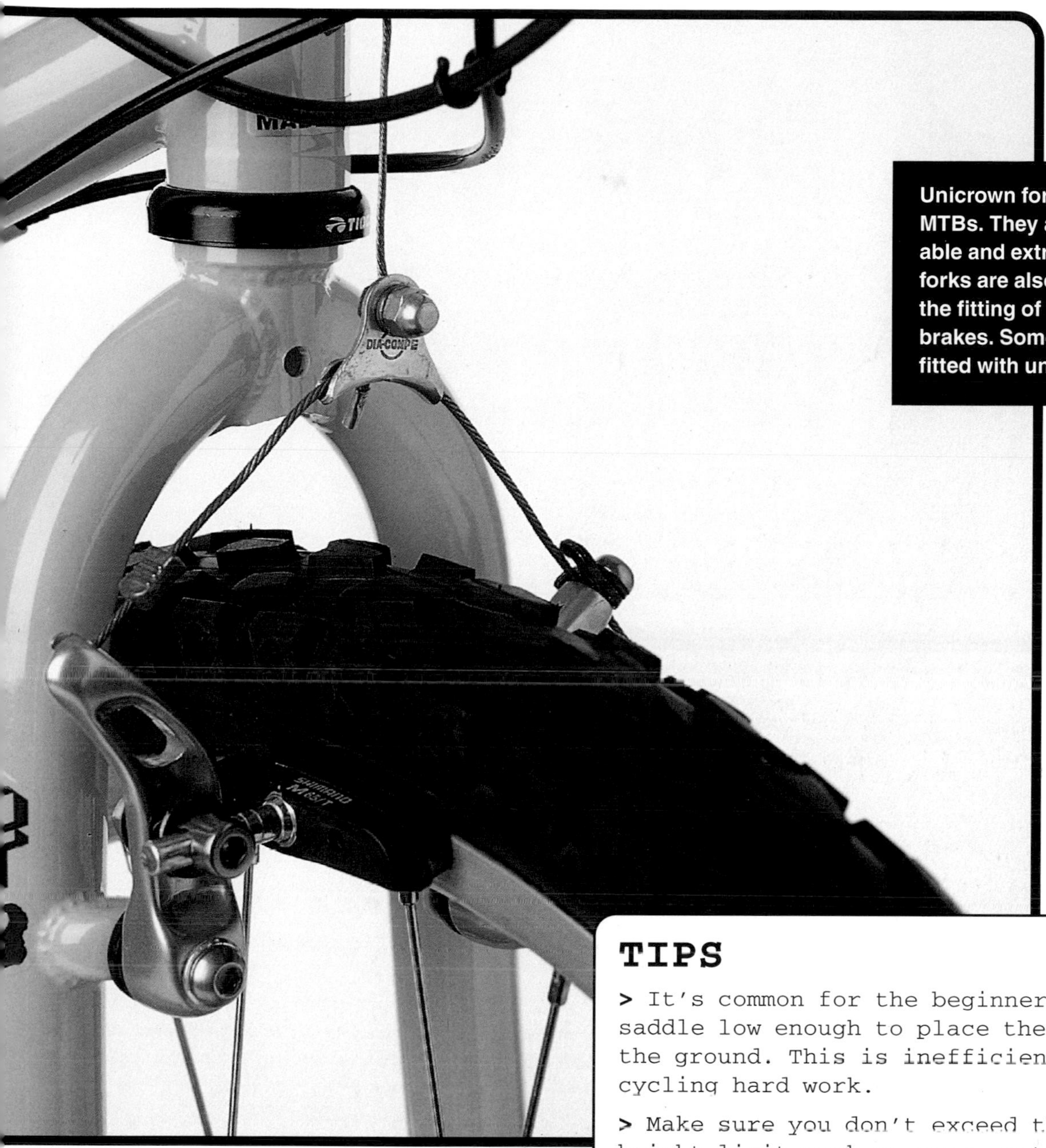

TIPS

> It's common for the beginner to have the saddle low enough to place the feet flat on the ground. This is inefficient and makes cycling hard work.

> Make sure you don't exceed the maximum height limit mark on your seatpost. If there isn't one, leave at least 2½ in of seatpost inside the frame.

Other considerations

Crank length is not crucial and most people will have no complaint with using standard 170mm or 175mm length cranks. However, competitive cyclists have realised a benefit from using alternative crank lengths. Our chart below gives recommendations.

Ideal road bike set-up

Inside leg	Saddle setback	Handlebar reach	Handlebar height	Crank length (mm)
72–75	3–5	42–50	4–5	160
75–78	4–6	46–55	5–6	162.5
79–82	5–7	49–57	6–7	165
83–86	6–8	52–59	7–8	170–172.5
87–90	7–9	54–60	8–9	175–177.5
91–94	8–10	57–63	9–10	180

(All measurements, except crank length, are in cm)

BIKE FRAMES

Lugs can be sculp-tured and chromed to great effect as on this Italian bike.

1. TIG welding is neat and minimizes heat damage to the tubing.

2. Fillet brazing produces a smooth joint.

3. Aluminium frames use the MIG welding process.

Frame construction

TIG welding
This method uses inexpensive materials and is used by almost all MTB manufacturers. The welded portion between the tubes is the filler metal – tungsten, which is welded with an inert gas to get a perfect join.

Lugged construction
The lugs provide a sandwich for the silver or brass brazing medium which holds the tubes together. This method of construction has been around for almost a century and remains popular in the frame building of road bikes.

Brazing
This is where the metal used to join the tubes is different from the material the tubes are made from. It is the most popular method of construction for custom frame builders and looks especially neat because the brazing medium, often silver, has a low melting point, limiting heat damage to the tubing.

Bonding
Single-mould carbon fibre frames are costly to produce. Bonding carbon tubes together using lugs is far cheaper. Bonded steel and aluminium frames have also been produced for road bikes in recent years.

Butting
Butted tubes are thinner in the centre section and thicker at the joint where the stress is most. This keeps weight to a minimum and maintains strength where its needed.

Frame materials

Steel
Steel is cheap and easy to build with and remains the most popular frame building material. The 'Hi-ten' label on some bikes denotes that it is made from high tensile steel tubing. Another popular steel mix is chromoly, which is made by alloying Chrome Molybdenum with steel. The results are lighter than Hi-ten. The alloying elements strengthen the steel so it can be made thinner thus saving weight. Chromoly is the popular choice for mid range MTBs and road bikes.

Aluminium
Large-diameter aluminium tubing looks heavy but generally results in a lighter frame than steel can offer. High end aluminium frames are particu-larly light and are butted to provide a responsive yet compliant ride which minimizes fatigue. The plain gauge tubes commonly seen on budget priced bikes weigh about the same as a steel frame, but they are stiffer, making them ideal for tall people.

Metal Matrix
An aluminium tube will break sooner than steel under a given amount of force. A metal matrix tube is basically an aluminium tube that has a

surface layer of ceramic particles to strengthen it, thus minimizing the chance of breakage following an accident. This makes it a better proposition than aluminium for the cut and thrust of massed start competition.

Carbon fibre

Carbon fibre is lighter than steel or alloy. The material is built up from resins and sheets of matting – just like a fibreglass boat hull. Comfort and stiffness is varied according to the number of sheets laid into the mould for the frame.

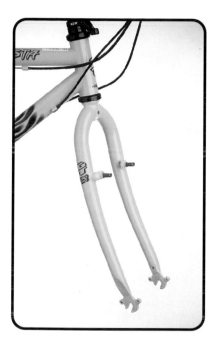

Titanium

Titanium is difficult to weld which is why it is so expensive. It also has a better life expectancy than any other frame material. Titanium frames such as the Merlin and Litespeed have a unique ride quality and are both comfortable and light.

Left: TIG welding is used on most steel MTB frames. It is cheap and very strong.

Above: The juncture of seat tube, chain stays and down tube has to withstand a great deal of pressure.

Above: Lugged construction has been used by frame makers for over a hundred years, but it remains popular. The lug strengthens the joint and provides a greater area for brazing.

LOOKING AFTER YOUR FRAME

Grade of job: Moderate.
Tools: Washing up brush, Proprietory solvent cleaner, Car accessory touch up paint, WD40.

Drainage holes

The area around the bottom bracket is the most prone to corrosion. It is here that water and condensation accumulate. Drill a small hole in the bottom bracket shell ⅛in diameter to provide a drain hole. Any water that gets into the hole has one exit – straight out again!

Frame protection

Owners of quality lightweight frames, especially MTBs, can protect the unpainted insides of their frames with an automotive underbody sealant compound of the type that flows freely into crevices, or a mineral oil of around 40w such as 2-stroke engine oil. But be careful…this increases the weight of your frame by about 40 grams!

1. Remove the bottom bracket unit (b/b) and forks.
2. Centrepunch the b/b shell and use a small starter drill. Then use a larger drill to at least ⅛in. Remove the burr on the inside of the b/b shell with a file or a blunt screwdriver.
3. Stuff newspaper into the business end of the seat tube and a piece of tape across the two vent holes inside the head tube.
4. With the bike upside-down place the straw which comes with the Waxoyl inside the seat tube and depress spray for about seven seconds. Repeat inside the down tube and chain stays. Stuff more newspaper into the bottom bracket shell and turn the frame a few times to disperse the Waxoyl evenly. Remove the newspaper and stand for at least two days to allow the excess sealant compound or oil to drain from the frame tubing before reassembly.

If you can't get the right colour to touch up your paintwork, use nail varnish instead.

Protect your frame by putting electricians' tape or a chainstay protection strip on the chainstay.

Damage to the chainstays

Examine the area of your frame adjacent to the chainrings. Damage can occur here due to 'chainsuck'. This is where the chain jams in the chainring teeth, and jams between the frame and the chain ring. A special device can reduce the chance of damage should this happen on your bike. There are several brands of anti-chainsuck device on the market – to fit one follow the two-point guide below.

1. Turn the bike upside down and offer up the anti-chainsuck device to the frame behind the bottom bracket. Place the fitting bolts through the appropriate holes (some have several), and hand tighten the bolts.

2. Be careful to align the device to avoid the control cables if fitted beneath the bottom bracket. Adjust the device so that the L-shaped cutouts are as close as possible to the chainring teeth without actually touching them. If it won't align with all three chainrings, get it as close as possible to the middle chainring. Fully tighten the fitting bolts and turn the cranks to confirm it doesn't touch the chainring teeth.

Touch up the paintwork

Inevitably chips will appear in the paintwork. It's unavoidable but easy to touch up…and it's important to do so before corrosion gets a hold.

1. Find a colour sample that is similar to that of your bike. Take it to an automotive supplier who will be able to get a close match with a tube of touch-up paint.

2. Wipe the area to be touched up with thinners then apply a small dab of paint to the area. Leave to dry before applying further dabs of paint until the touch up layers are higher than the rest of the paint.

3. Using wet and dry sandpaper, lightly sand your touch-up until it's flush with the rest of the paint, then use a light rubbing compound to shine.

Scratch prevention

Superficial scratches can be prevented by using clear waterproof tape – sometimes used for gardening. Placed along the top tube and areas where the cables chafe on the frame, it will protect your valuable paintwork for years.

Protect the insides of your frame by using an automotive underbody compound.

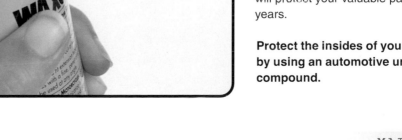

THE HEADSET

The headset controls the movement of the fork. It contains ball bearings or roller bearings that must be kept properly adjusted for the steering to remain true. There are two basic types of headset: the threaded type, which fit onto a fork with a threaded steerer tube, and the threadless kind which adjust by Allen bolt.

Headset components

> The crown race: This fits over the fork crown and usually has a weather seal to protect the bearings.
> Bearings: The roller type crown bearings have a larger surface area than the commonly used ball bearing race so they last longer.
> Upper and lower cups: These fit into the frame and cup the bearings.

Dimensions

> Sizes: There are three common headset sizes, 1in, 1⅛ in and 1¼ in, which is sometimes called 'Evolution' size though is no longer used on production frames.
> Stack height: The stack height is the amount of steerer length which the headset occupies. It is measured from the base of the crown race to the inside edge of the locking nut on the upper stack.

Use an Allen key (usually a 6mm) to secure the stem to the fork steerer.

TIP

> If you are buying a replacement headset by mail order you will be asked which size and type you require. If in doubt contact the main supplier of your brand of bike; a cycling magazine will be able to help with a contact number.

Right: If you're fitting new forks make sure the top of the fork steerer tube is at least 2mm beneath the top of the A-head stem as shown here.

Left: Use a 5mm Allen key to remove any detectable play in the steering.

Headset adjustment

Grade of job: Moderato.
Tools: A threadless headset requires 6mm and 5mm Allen keys while conventional headsets require a pair of headset spanners.

Threaded headset

1. Place your thumb and forefinger around the lower stack of the headset, then, using your right hand, apply the front brake and push fore and aft. If there is play detectable, slacken the uppermost nut on the headset stack, then turn the nut beneath it clockwise until you feel resistance.
2. Using a spanner to hold the lower nut in position, tighten the upper nut down onto the lower nut. Keeping the upper nut stationary, turn the lower nut anti-clockwise until it will move no further.

Threadless headset:

1. The most commonly used threadless headset has a 5mm bolt in the top and usually a 5mm Allen headed side bolt. Another popular headset is the Diatech which uses a single Allen bolt to adjust the bearings.
2. If you can detect play using the same method as described in point 1 for the threaded headset, slacken the side bolt, then turn the top bolt about one-eighth of a turn. Check that your handlebars are straight before fully tightening the side bolt.

Re-greasing the headset

Grade of job: Moderate.

Headset bearings, although sealed, are prone to corrosion caused by spray kicked up by the front wheel. This can be prevented by regular greasing. Follow the three-point guide below to check your headset bearings:

1. Remove the front wheel and turn the handlebars left to right. Any roughness will be immediately felt and warrants some further investigation.
2. Place the bike in a workstand.
   In the case of a threaded headset, loosen the upper locking nut, then undo the stem bolt and tap it with a hammer to release the wedge. Lift the handlebars free. When holding the forks, strike the steerer using a soft hammer to free the forks from the headset.
   In the case of a threadless headset, undo the top and side Allen headed bolts.
   Lift the handlebars free.
3. In the case of a threaded headset, hold the forks whilst removing the upper lock ring followed by the locking washer and the adjuster cup. Wipe the grease and grime from the bearing tracks and examine the bearings. Replace them if even slightly rusty. There are no common sizes for headset bearings, so take an old bearing to the shop for replacements.

HANDLEBARS AND STEM

Grade of job: Moderate.
Tools: 5 and 6mm Allen keys. Use the appropriate Allen key for grip shift. Screwdriver, Spray oil or washing-up liquid, Copper Eze or waterproof grease.

By wedging the stem open with a large screwdriver you can prevent scratching the handlebars. Never force the handlebars into a tight stem – if in doubt get advice regarding compatabilty from a reputable shop.

Handlebar reach

Handlebar reach is a matter of personal preference, though as a guide weight should be evenly distributed between the saddle and the handlebar. There is a vast range of stems available, all of which will effect your riding position and thereby comfort. Many riders replace conventional drop handlebars with the anatomic variety – which have flat, rather than curved, handholds. Seek advice from a shop before embarking on this change as the reach and width measurements differ from model to model, often requiring a new stem to achieve the same handlebar reach.

Whatever set-up you choose, aim to get a position that's comfortable on the drops and also on the tops of the bars. See the chart on page 161 for a guide to handlebar height and reach for road bikes.

MTB manufacturers have spent years getting the handlebar set-up right for the mass market and, provided your bike shop has advised you correctly regarding the size of bike,

you're unlikely to gain any significant advantage by changing the manufacturer's stem. Downhill racers favour a stem that's usually 3cm shorter than a cross-country stem. Riders with back problems may also want to change their stem. If you do need a longer/shorter stem, there is a vast range available.

TIPS

> The force exerted on a bar end during a spill can result in a crimped handlebar. The damaged portion of the tube can be trimmed with a hacksaw though, of course, this narrows your bars considerably.

> To avoid confusion when ordering a new quill stem, look for the size stamped on the stem, 25.4mm refers to 1in, 30.2mm refers to 1¹/₈in and there's Evolution 1¹/₄in. A-head stems are available in either 1in or 1¹/₈in.

Handlebar height

The difference between the distance from the ground to the top of the saddle and the distance from the ground to the top of the handlebars is your handlebar height. Most handlebar stems are adjustable through 2cm. For the most aerodynamic position you need to be as low as possible but this can be a strain on your back, so let your muscles get used to the position before you take on a long ride. Downhill MTB racers and beginners often prefer a higher handlebar height – handlebars with the 'DH' prefix have an upward bend and are recommended.

(See page 161 for the chart concerning handlebar height for road bikes.)

Inspection and stem replacement

1. If a stem is cracked as a result of an accident, inspect all welds closely for similar damage.
2. Remove the grips. Poke a screwdriver behind the grip and squirt with a thin lube, work the blade round the grip and pull with a twisting motion. Remove the brake and gear levers.
3. To remove an A-head type stem, undo the top Allen bolt followed by the side bolt, lift the stem and handlebar assembly from the fork steerer and take care not to loose the spacers if fitted.
4. To remove a quill-type stem leave the handlebar in position, turn the Allen head bolt anti-clockwise and lift the handlebar/stem assembly together.
5. To fit a new A-head stem, use the correct number of spacer washers to achieve the correct fork steerer overlap. Fit the handlebars and controls and tighten them enough to prevent them turning – though no further.
6. Quill stems should be greased before fitting. Coat the sliding surfaces of the wedge, the threads of the bolt and the underside of the bolt head. Don't forget to coat the outside of the wedge to prevent corrosion.

Above: Never exceed the maximum height mark on the quill of the stem.

Right: It's vital to check the stem is tight. Support the wheel with your legs and try to twist the bars. See point 5, right.

Below: Crimped handlebars are dangerous. Trim off the damaged portion of the bars with a hacksaw.

Don't expect your handlebars and stem to last forever. Handlebar and stem breakages aren't uncommon and you should always inspect yours after a heavy spill.

SEAT POSTS

Grade of job: Potentially hard.
Tools: 5mm and 6mm Allen key, Penetrating oil, Ruler or flat edge, Grease.

Seat posts are commonly made from aluminium which is unprotected and prone to corrosion. To prevent movement the seat post must be a tight fit in the frame. Grease applied around the post stops corrosion and prevents the post getting stuck.

Unseizing the seatpost: Remove the saddle and, using the frame as a lever, apply a twisting motion to free the seatpost.

Check before you buy

Before buying a second-hand bike, try lifting the seatpost. In extreme cases an oxyacetylene torch will be needed to remove the post – if this proves to be the case, your bike may well need a respray.

Unseizing the seatpost

If your seatpost cannot be removed by manipulating the saddle, don't reach straight for the matches and the oxyacetylene torch...try the following approach.

1. Remove the bottom bracket unit and, with the bike inverted, spray some freeing oil down the seat tube. Leave to soak for at least 24 hours.
2. Remove both the wheels and the saddle, then clamp the top of the seatpost in the jaws of a vice. If the seatpost is of the type with a separate steel saddle clasp, cut the narrow section at the top and place a short piece of steel rod or a socket into the tube, before clamping the seatpost.
   Using the frame as a lever, turn and lift the bike simultaneously to release the seatpost. If this doesn't work, strip the bike entirely, after which the frame will have to be entrusted to a frame builder who will melt the seatpost out of the frame using a torch.
3. Before fitting a replacement seatpost, coat the outside surface with an anti-seize compound or grease. Fresh grease should be applied every three months.

TIP

> If you need a longer seatpost be sure to state the diameter required, as there are many sizes. It's usually stamped on the side of the tube; 27.2mm is a common size. If it isn't marked, seek advice from a bike shop.

Saddles

Saddle choice is a personal thing and experienced cyclists tend to favour particular brands or models. The Selle Italia Flite is exceptionally popular amongst male riders. Many novice riders replace their saddle in the mistaken belief that it will reduce the soreness they are experiencing. In most cases, careful positioning of the saddle and padded cycling shorts would have helped more. However, many saddles supplied with new bikes are commonly unsuitable for women riders. Saddles available specifically for the needs of women have wider rear sections or cutaways; the Terry range of women's saddles is very popular.

Place the bike on a flat surface and rest a ruler along the saddle. Loosen the Allen bolts beneath the saddle if it's not level.

TIP

> If your bike has a cheap steel saddle clasp it's likely that the saddle will dip, especially on an MTB. The long term answer is to replace it with a micro-adjusting seat post.

Adjusting your saddle

1. Adjust the angle of your saddle so that it is perfectly horizontal, then firmly tighten the bolt or clasp.
2. Make sure your saddle is at the right height. As a rough guide, you should have a slight bend in your knee when your heel is on the pedal at its lowest point. More precisely, establish your inside leg measurement and multiply it by 1.07. See page 161, saddle setback, for the appropriate fore/aft position of the saddle.
3. Loosen the clamp bolt at the top of the seat tube and using a tape measure adjust the saddle height so that it matches your calculation – measure from the centre of the bottom bracket to the top of the saddle. If the correct saddle height exceeds the height limit mark of your seatpost you will have to obtain a longer seatpost.
4. Tighten the bolt at the top of the seat tube, then check it's secure by forcing the saddle with your hands.

Above: Firmly tighten the cradle bolt using an Allen key with good leverage.

Right: Never exceed the maximum height mark shown on the side of the seatpost.

MAINTAINING CLIPPED PEDALS

Grade of job: Hard.
Tools: Appropriate spanner to remove the locknut (usually 8mm or 10mm),
Small screwdriver, No1 pozidrive screwdriver or 4/5mm Allen key, Grease gun,
Pedal bearings.

Clipped and strapped pedals are simple devices. But watch out for loose attachment screws and regrease the bearings at regular intervals – especially after wet rides.

Clipped pedals are supplied as original equipment on most MTBs, but some, mainly the resin-bodied type, aren't sealed from the elements.

Resin-bodied pedals aren't worth stripping down to repair if the bearings become stiff – not least because the cageplates aren't removable to gain access to the bearings. They are also relatively cheap to replace. If, however, your pedals are of aluminium and steel construction, they are worth servicing for long life. To inspect the bearings follow the following sequence.

1. Unscrew the bolts which secure the cageplate and place the bolts in a safe place.
2. Prise off, or in the case of many road pedals, screw-off the end cap.
3. Using the axle to hold it, place the pedal in a vice and turn the outermost axle nut anti-clockwise, followed by the tab washer and the adjuster cone.
4. Grasp the axle between thumb and forefinger then remove the pedal from the jaws of the vice. Place the pedal into a plastic bag and invert it. The ball bearings will fall out, together with the axle.
   Clean and inspect the parts the ball bearings run through for pitting marks. The axle is most prone to problems.
5. Always fit new bearings; they cost little and the old ones will almost certainly have a degree of wear. Take the old ones to your bike shop to match replacements.
6. Use grease to hold the bearings in place. Position the axle on the vice and carefully place the pedal body over it. Replace the adjuster cone turning it clockwise until it's just seated, then back it off a little. Fit the tab washer (where needed), and the lock nut. Tighten the locknut fully, then grasp the pedal to check the bearings for play. If the bearings are tight or won't turn at all, loosen the locknut and turn the adjuster cone anti-clockwise a little. Tighten the locknut again. If the bearings are loose, turn the adjuster cone clockwise.
7. If there isn't one already, drill a small hole about 1.5mm into the dustcap end of the pedal then apply some grease through the hole using a miniature grease gun.
8. If you're just regreasing the pedals, pump the unit until the old grease is purged out around the innermost part of the axle.

Regular mainte nance would have prevented the bearing cup on this pedal from becoming corroded and pitting badly.

Above: The small bearing surface area of this axle means the bearing lands have worn rapidly.

Right: Pedal components are tiny so be sure to put the parts in a safe place when you strip the pedal for servicing.

JARGON BUSTER

> Cageplate: this is the part that your soles grip.

> Bearing lands: these are the parts of the pedal that the bearings run through. In this case they are in the pedal body and the axle.

> Adjuster cone: this is the bit that screws down onto the axle, allowing fine adjustment of the bearings.

MAINTAINING SPD PEDALS

Grade of job: Difficult.
Tools: Vice or molegrips, 6mm spanner or small adjustable, 10mm open ended spanner, Pozidrive or Philips screwdriver, Very small flat-bladed screwdriver, Grey Shimano special tool, 44 x ³⁄₃₂in ball bearings.

Road bike clipless pedals seem to go on for ever, but the off road pedals require regular maintenance to keep the bearings running smoothly. The ubiquitous Shimano SPD pedal is covered here and yes, there's a use for that grey plastic ring thing that is supplied with the pedals.

1. Clear the mud from the pedal using an old spoke and wash the remainder using degreaser.
2. Place the bearing removal tool (the grey plastic object that comes with the pedals) over the right-hand pedal axle and cramp the tool in the jaws of a vice, then grasp the pedal body, turning it clockwise to unscrew the axle assembly. Turn the left-hand pedal anti-clockwise to remove the axle assembly.
3. Position the axle in the vice. Loosen the lock nut with a 6mm spanner followed by the tab washer and cone. Place the bearing assembly in a container then lift the sleeve from the

Above: Using the special tool, turn the axle assembly into the body of the pedal. Place the tool in a vice and use the body of the pedal to tighten, but don't use excessive force.

axle. The bearings will fall out. Inspect the bearing lands on the axle for serious pitting marks. Keep the bearing retainer sleeve with the axle you removed it from and inspect the delicate plastic thread for damage. Replace with an aftermarket aluminium version if

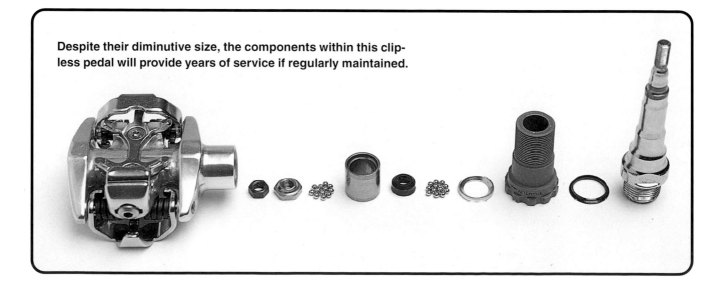

Despite their diminutive size, the components within this clipless pedal will provide years of service if regularly maintained.

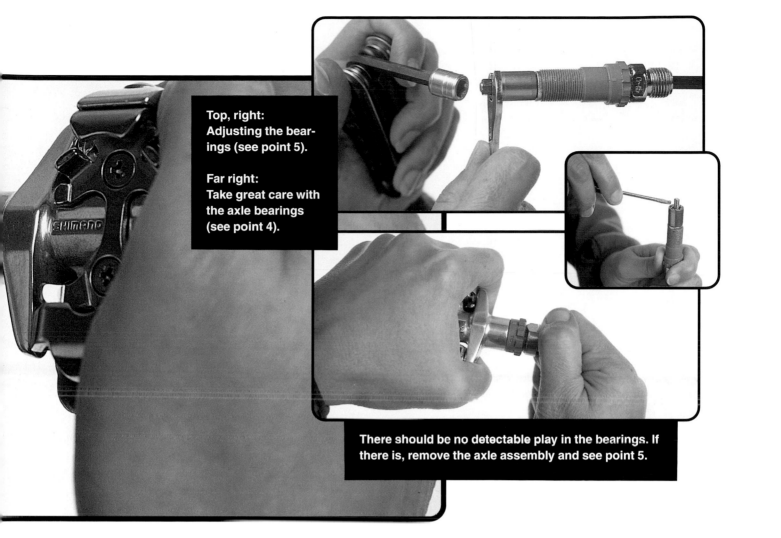

Top, right:
Adjusting the bearings (see point 5).

Far right:
Take great care with the axle bearings (see point 4).

There should be no detectable play in the bearings. If there is, remove the axle assembly and see point 5.

there's damage or you've had to melt it to get the axle assembly out (see tips).

4. Pop the plastic sleeve over the axle followed by the narrow washer – fit this with the chamfer uppermost then apply a sticky grease, like Mobil HP222 or Shimano Pro Line, to the axle and place the ³⁄₃₂ in ball bearings around the washer. Slide the metal sleeve over the axle and place the plastic tube through it. Place further ³⁄₃₂ in bearings around the outside edge of the sleeve followed by the cone, tab washer and the locknut.

5. Using a 10mm spanner to hold the adjuster cone, adjust the bearings so there's detectable play when the sleeve is moved and then tighten the locknut firmly, using a 6mm spanner.

6. Squeeze some grease into the pedal body before fitting the axle assembly. Carefully insert and screw in the axle (see tips below), then tighten firmly using the tool. If the bearings feel rough, remove the axle assembly and slacken the locking nut, then turn the adjuster cone about one eighth anticlockwise. Finally, tighten the lock nut firmly down onto the adjuster cone.

TIPS

> When replacing the axle assembly into the right-hand pedal, turn the body of the pedal clockwise.

> If the pedal turns without unscrewing, the thread has stripped. Put the pedal axle in the vice and heat the body of the pedal using a butane torch. When the plastic bearing retainer starts to bubble, lift the pedal away from the axle, using molegrips. Avoid breathing the fumes.This procedure requires great care.

> If you have to melt the axle assembly out find a well ventilated area and open the windows, as the fumes are toxic.

> Don't try to remove the springs within the SPD mechanism – there's no need and it's the devil's work to re-fit them.

> The four cross headed retainer plate screws on XT SPDs have a habit of disappearing. Use a drop of glue on them to prevent them loosening.

> Use molegrips to hold the special tool if you don't have access to a vice; use your feet to stop the grips moving around.

TROUBLESHOOTING

Symptom	Cause
Saddle soreness	Saddle not level/Wrong type of saddle
Bike uncomfortable	Cramped or stretched position
Wrists ache	Cramped position
Bike feels vague and difficult to steer	Tight steering bearings or loose spokes
Gears click	Cable stretched
Chain won't go onto small chainring	Maladjusted gear
Chain falls off repeatedly	Maladjusted gear
Bike vibrates when brakes applied	Dented or out of true wheel
Squeaking noise on each pedal revolution	Loose crank arm
Light click on each pedal revolution	Stiff chain link
Frequent punctures	Insufficient air in tyres/Foreign object in tyre carcass
Knocking noise over uneven surfaces	Headset loose
Bike pulls to one side	Forks or possibly frame bent

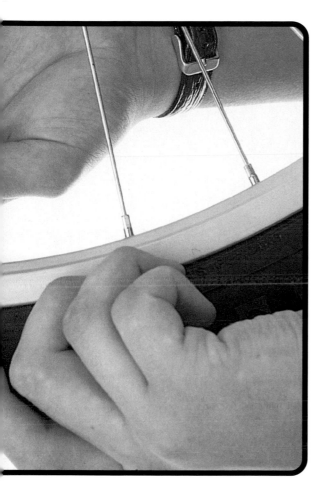

Remedy	See page...
Loosen clamp and adjust until level/ Change saddle	171
Move saddle or change the stem	171
Change the stem	168
Adjust steering. Adjust spoke tension.	122 and 168
Pull cable through gear mech	140
Adjust low limit gear screw	140
Adjust low or high limit screw	140
True wheel using spoke key	122
Tighten crank	146
Manipulate the chain with your thumbs or use the upper portion of a chain tool	150
Inflate tyres and use tyre gauge/Remove foreign objects with a dull knife blade	120
Adjust using headset spanner	166
New frame/forks	Buy new frame/forks

UPGRADE YOUR MTB

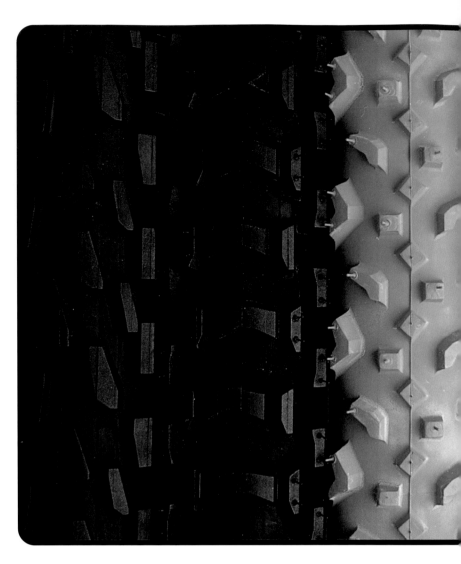

The better your bike is, the more you will want to use it. The majority of low end bikes use heavy, basic equipment and are ripe for upgrading. However, if your bike has steel rims and a high tensile steel frame it's better to consider a new bike if you want to spend your weekends racing or riding in the hills.

Bar ends are a popular MTB upgrade. They enable you to vary your riding position and help reduce the pressure on your forearms.

Suspension fork

Above all other upgrades, suspension forks will make riding easier. They minimize fatigue and help you maintain control when descending. The only downside is that they add weight.

Rating 5/5

Bar ends

Bar ends give you an extra handhold that's ideal for traversing hills when you have to get out of the saddle. They are also great for easing the pressure on the forearms caused by long hours spent riding in one position. Valuable on the road. Bar ends come in several lengths.

Rating 3/5

Toeclips and straps

Toeclips and straps help to keep your feet in the best position and provide support when pulling the pedals on a climb. It's a misconception that you can't get your feet out of the straps. In the event of a fall the straps have enough give to allow the foot to release.

They're not ideal for racing as your feet can slip out of them on off-road surfaces. Another bonus is that they don't clog up with mud.

Rating 4/5

Top left: MTB tryes come in all manner of shapes and sizes. Soft, coloured, knobbly tyres look great, but are not suited for tarmac riding. Slick and semi-slick tyres (above) are best for road riding. They offer better cornering grip and less rolling resistance.

Left: Titanium and suspension specific hubs are an excellent 'high end' upgrade.

Saddle

An upgrade to an expensive saddle will not cure saddle soreness. Instead, spend your money on a good pair of cycling shorts.

However, most mid to high end bikes are supplied with narrow saddles which are commonly unsuitable for women. The Terry range of saddles are anatomically shaped to suit the female pelvis and have been widely acclaimed in the cycling press.

Rating 3/5

Clipless pedals

If you already use clips and straps you will know that they take some getting used to and are difficult to get your feet into in a hurry. Clipless pedals are easier to use and are particularly valuable when hopping over obstacles. On the downside, they are expensive as you'll need a pair of compatible shoes which allow a cleat to be fitted to the soles.

Rating 5/5

Reflective tape

Remove your reflectors and replace them with reflective tape. It's more effective and you'll save about 180g.

Rating 3/5

Latex inner tubes

Save the all important rotating weight and get an inner tube you can always repair into the bargain. Latex tubes are around 50g lighter and accept puncture repairs far more readily than the butyl variety.

Rating 4/5

SUSPENSION

Suspension forks are amongst the most popular MTB upgrades and, if working properly, they should take some of the shock that would otherwise be absorbed by the frame and tyres alone. The most common suspension forks are the telescopic type. They have a lower and upper part which slide into each other under the pressure of a spring or a compressible plastic stack called an elastomer. The spring rate of a fork is determined by the presence of grease which eventually displaces through normal use. To maintain performance this grease must be replenished.

Suspension without bounce

The fork has a dampening property to slow down the rate that it reacts to sudden movements. If it didn't, your bike would become more like a pogo stick. Most forks also have a dampener adjustment dial which dictates the speed with which the fork reacts to different surfaces. Forks can thus be tailored for rider weight and terrain.

Suspension facts

Air/oil forks use coil steel springs and a series of valves which oil is forced through as the fork compresses and rebounds.

Full suspension bikes have a rear-mounted shock unit pivoting on a swinging rear fork. Creaking sounds usually result from friction between two moving surfaces – usually around the rear fork pivot bushes. To cure this, grease the surfaces.

If you are dismantling the forks always turn the top cap in an anti-clockwise direction.

Hydraulic forks require air. Refer to the manufacturers recommendations.

Servicing elastomer forks

Elastomer forks require re-greasing after every six hours of continuous riding. Before servicing, check for wear. Apply the front brake and rock the bike fore and aft. If there's play accompanied by a clunking sound, take your bike to a dealer for further inspection. He may suggest replacement of the fork bushes for which special tools are required. If there's little or no play, follow the following six-point guide.

Grade of job: Hard.
Tools: 4mm and 5mm hex keys, Special fork grease, Piece of doweling and a rag.

1. Don't remove the fork brace, there's no need. To separate the upper and lower legs of the fork, insert a 5mm Allen key into the bolts at the bottom of each leg. Get a friend to compress the forks if the bolts are just turning.
2. After removing the bolts, pull the lower tubes free from the upper tubes.
3. Clean the aluminium upper tubes and the bushing surfaces inside the magnesium lower tubes using a rag and degreaser to shift the spent grease.
4. Loosen the 4mm or 5mm crown bolts, then unscrew the top cap assembly (turning anti-clockwise) and drop the skewer, MCU (Micro Cellular Urethane spring) and springs out, it helps to tilt the bike upside down as they'll stay on the skewer. Clean the skewer with a rag.
5. Apply a light coating of the special grease called JUDY Butter to the lower tube bushings; use a piece of doweling or a coat hanger to reach the bushings. Grease the aluminium skewer, then reinstall the springs, being sure to use a spacer between each spring.
6. Screw the adjuster cap/MCU skewer back into the upper tube of the fork, then fit the fork boots. Reinstall the upper tubes into the crown and apply locking agent to the crown bolt threads. Tighten firmly (5ft/lb if you have a torque wrench).

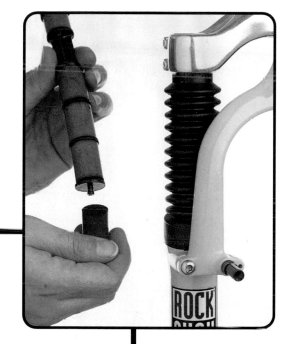

Left: The MCU or Micro Cellular Urethane spring in this Rock Shox Judy fork have tiny air bubbles which provide different springing characteristics to the elastomer springs which are shown on the left of the picture.

Left: The oil required for the fork should be measured out carefully.

ROAD BIKE UPGRADES

Whether you're replacing worn parts or upgrading to save weight, fun can be had tracking down the best components and making your bike better to ride. There are plenty of brightly coloured CNC milled and anorexic-looking gizmos out there...the hard part is working out which ones will be useful for the sort of cycling you do.

Upgrading for weight

Upgrades that reduce rotating weight, like tyres and wheels, have more of an effect on performance than changes to other components.

Upgrading for comfort

For touring, upgrades should be aimed at improving comfort and convenience. Road bikes are often supplied with a short stem – a longer stem will be needed for a typical touring set-up. Combined control levers, such as Campag Ergopower or Shimano STI, can improve pedalling efficiency by encouraging gear changing – it also means you don't have to grope around trying to find those downtube shifters. A strong rack or anatomically shaped handlebars also improve comfort.

Cycle computer

A cycle computer is the most cost effective upgrade you can make. For a minimal outlay you can gauge your mileage and speed. A computer is an invaluable aid for anyone wishing to get into touring or competitive cycling.

Rating 5/5

The frame

The frame is the heart of the bicycle so it needs to be right for you and your riding. If your bike has a Reynolds, Columbus or Oria label you already have a frame made from excellent tubing. There are many other types of quality tubing, so get advice from a shop that has a reputation for its road bikes.

Rating 5/5

Cycle computers are easy to fit and essential if you are going to train or race. Even the most basic computer will tell you your current speed, average speed and trip distance.

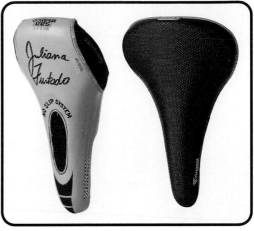

Above: special saddles are designed for the needs of the female cyclist.

Left: Mass produced road bikes are often supplied with cheap tyres. An upgrade to a quality tyre with a Kevlar layer will improve your speed and cornering confidence. It will also help you avoid punctures.

Below: Combined brake/gear levers are an expensive upgrade.

Tyres

Along with the saddle, your tyres determine ride comfort. A good tyre conforms to road surfaces better than a cheap tyre so you go faster. It will also be more predictable. Some tyres have a Kevlar layer which resists intrusions better than others – extremely valuable for touring.

Rating 4/5

Spokes

Lightweight butted spokes save about 50g per wheel of rotating weight. Worth it if your bike has plain gauge spokes.

Rating 3/5

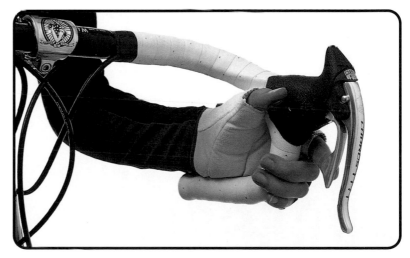

Clipless pedals

Almost every serious road cyclist uses clipless pedals. The Look and Time range are easy to get in and out of and are slightly safer in the event of a spill than clips and straps. Clipless pedals also give you more pedal power by enabling you to pull harder on the pedals – particularly valuable when climbing.

Rating 4/5

Shifters

Campag Ergopower and Shimano STI offer a far more convenient way of changing gear as you don't have to take your hands away from the handlebars. The downside is that they weigh more than conventional shifters mounted on the down tube.

Rating 5/5

FITTING ACCESSORIES

Accessories such as lights, cycle computers, mudguards and racks will make your bike more versatile. Fitting instructions can look daunting, but in most cases accessories are pretty simple to fit.

TIPS

> Keep your receipt in case there's something missing.

> Get an idea of what the thing looks like in an assembled state – either from a photograph or, ideally, fitted on to another bike.

> Check all the parts are in the pack before you start fitting.

Cycle computer

Fitting a cycle computer

1. Secure the cable next to the computer head with a tie wrap to prevent it pulling.
2. Route the wires carefully and check they don't stretch when the steering is turned to extremes.
3. The cable tie wraps used for securing the cables can be bought separately from an electrical wholesaler. Use tape if you wish.
4. The Avocet range of cycle computers use magnets which attach to the hub of most wheels – ideal for wheels with no spokes to mount a magnet.
5. Be careful when turning the plastic 'hose clamp' type screws on some sensors; tighten them enough to prevent the sensor moving and no more.
6. If you have to calculate the wheel circumference, mark the tyre and the ground with

correction fluid, turn the wheel one full revolution and measure the distance travelled.

7. Closely trim the cable ties as the edges can cause grazes to the hands when cleaning the bike.
8. Though most cycle computers are claimed to be waterproof this isn't always the case – in wet weather cover the computer head with cling film.

Make sure bolts securing the tri bars to the handlebars are tightened firmly. Use the correct Allen key for the job.

Fitting tri bars

1. If your bike is on the large side for you, buy tri bars that can be fitted beneath the handlebars, e.g. Mavic and Profile brands.
2. Read the instructions and use the bolt that's appropriate to that part of the bar – the fitting clamps have threads that are easily stripped if you use a bolt with a short thread.
3. If the tri bars move on the clamps when fully tightened, remove the anodising on the

mating surfaces of the handlebar using sandpaper or emery cloth and place a little locking agent on the mating surfaces before reassembly.

4. Bar end shifters such as the Shimano Ultegra can be fitted into the ends of most tri bars.
5. If the arm rests prove to be inadequate, replacements in various thickness of polystyrene foam can be purchased.

PUMP TIP

> If your pump has become ineffective, remove the screw cap and withdraw the plunger, then apply a little grease to the inside of the barrel before putting it back together. If the washer on the end of the plunger is made of leather, flatten it before greasing.

Tips for fitting mudguards

1. Ensure all fitting bolts clear the chain.
2. Don't fit the mudguard bridge in such a way that it pulls the mudguard upwards. Use the stays to manipulate the mudguards to the profile that you want.
3. If you want to connect a dynamo, use mudguards with built-in wire strips ready to connect to the rear light.
4. Trim the stays using the portion of a combination plier that's intended for cutting wire. Mudguard kits usually include black plastic protector caps for the stays.
5. If your bike doesn't have any mudguard eyes you can fit specially designed vinyl-coated brackets. Install them on the stays just above the dropouts.

Tips on lights

1. Get a front light that fits your bike. Some fitting brackets foul the control cables – a particular problem for some MTBs and road bikes with Campagnolo Ergopower levers.
2. Get a rear light that fits without sacrificing other accessories. If you already have a saddle wedgepack, get a lamp that fits on the seatpost, beneath the wedgepack.
3. Secure the lamp fitting bracket firmly to prevent the lamp shifting over uneven road surfaces.
4. Batteries don't last forever – always carry spares.
5. Batteries leak – take the batteries out of your lights if you're not going to be using them for a few weeks or more.
6. Always carry a spare bulb if you use a dynamo.

Bags and packs

1. A pack that fits around the waist with a belt closure is useful for carrying keys, spare inner tube and food. This type of bag is especially effective as it doesn't effect the handling properties of the bike.
2. If you don't want anything round your waist, consider a wedge pack. They come in a wide range of sizes – but check there's enough room for your rear light if you mount it on the seatpost.
3. Handlebar-mounted bags are a convenient way to carry essential items. They usually have a map pocket which is useful for long rides.
4. Panniers offer a large carrying capacity and make the bicycle a genuine option for weekly shopping trips.
5. The cycle trailer offers the greatest carrying capacity. It's usually a plastic box with a lockable lid, the connection to the bike being made with an arm attached to the chainstay and rear axle.

Left: Use pliers to trim the mudguard stays.

Right: U locks are heavy. It's safer and more comfortable to carry them on the frame than in a bag or on a rack.

Locks

1. The more you spend on a lock the better the level of protection.
2. Get one which fits your bike without fouling the controls. The best place to store a lock is beneath the top tube.
3. Avoid flimsy looking chain locks that cost a few pounds. They provide little, if any, protection from theft.
4. U locks provide the best protection, though get one that's long enough to go through the frame and around some street furniture.
5. Keep the lock working smoothly with a squirt of spray oil.

GLOSSARY

A

Aerobic exercise
Endurance-type exercise in which your lungs supply oxygen to your muscles.

Anaerobic exercise
Intense exercise, such as sprinting, which is above your **maximum heart rate** and doesn't use oxygen. Capable of being sustained for only a few minutes.

Aerodynamic drag
How much the air slows you down. Drag is the main force that stops a cyclist going faster, hence the smooth Lycra clothes, aerodynamic racing tucks, and **drafting**.The effort needed to overcome drag increases at the cube of your speed, so to go from 24mph to 30mph, it takes not 25% more power but 95% more!

Alloy A mixture of metals. Steel can be used alloyed (as **chromoly** steel) or on its own – though it is rather heavy like this. Lighter metals such as aluminium and titanium must be alloyed to improve strength.

Ankling Paddling the foot up and down from the ankle while pedalling, so distributing your power over more of the pedal stroke. Most effective while climbing or pedalling at a low cadence.

Audax Also known as a reliability ride or a randonée, an Audax is essentially a non-competitive **time trial** for touring cyclists. Riders have to complete a set distance – 50km and upwards – within a certain time limit. The Paris-Brest-Paris is the original and most famous.

B

Banking The steeply sloping bends on a cycle track.

Bearings Bikes use ball bearings of various sizes in the headset, hub axles, freewheel, pedals and bottom bracket. Sometimes they're loose, sometimes set in a cage or race. Fit-and-forget sealed cartridge bearings, which incorporate the moving parts in one disposable unit, are now common. Some headsets incorporate roller bearings, while cheap bikes may use ineffective sleeve bearings, or bushings.

Bonk Also known as 'hunger knock', bonking is caused by a low blood sugar level. It results in light-headedness and a lack of energy.

Break A small group of riders that escapes from the **bunch** in a massed start race.

Bunch The main group of riders in a massed start race. Cyclists take turns at the front, then drop back and **draft** to save energy. A bunch is capable of moving faster than a lone rider or **break**.

Butted tubing Tubing which is internally thicker at the stressed tube ends than in the middle. It gives the same strength tube for less weight. Spokes may also be butted.

Braze-ons Non-structural 'extras' on a frame, including bosses for bottle cages or gear levers, and eyelets for racks or mudguards.

Brazing Like soldering, but a lot hotter, brazing joins two steel surfaces together with another metal that has a lower melting point, such as brass.

C

Cable housing The plastic-covered, coiled steel tubes which enable the tensioned brake and gear cables inside to pass round bends.

Cadence Pedalling rate. The optimum cadence is between 80 and 110rpm.

Chromoly Steel alloyed with chrome and molybdenum, giving greater strength for less weight.

Cleat Metal or plastic plate used to lock a cycle shoe to the pedal.

Clipless pedals Pedals with sprung, ski-type bindings, which lock a dedicated **cleat** to the pedal. As a rule, clipless pedals cannot be ridden with ordinary shoes.

Crank The lever that connects the pedal to the bottom bracket and the chainring.

D

Dished wheel
Derailleur-geared rear wheels are dished, meaning the spokes on the cassette side are shorter and angled more steeply than on the other side, so that there is room for the cassette between the drop outs. Front wheels and hub-geared wheels are symmetrical.

Disc wheel Solid wheel which is heavier but more aerodynamic than a spoked wheel. Dangerous in crosswinds.

Drafting Riding in the slipstream of another rider to save energy.

Drop outs Where the wheel axles bolt into the frame.

Drops Slang for dropped bars, or specifically the lower part of such bars.

E

Energy drink Drink with added sugars, vitamins and minerals. Useful for keeping your blood sugar and energy levels up to avoid the **bonk**, as well as providing fluid.

F

Fixed gear Also known as fixed wheel, a fixed gear bike is one on which you cannot freewheel, such as a track bike.

Freehub A hub with an integral freewheel. Also known as a cassette hub.

Freewheel Mechanism of bearings, pawls and ratchets. When freewheeling (rolling without pedalling), the pawls slide over the ratchets, giving a distinctive clicking sound. When pedalling, the pawls engage the ratchets, driving the wheel. Screw-on freewheels have been made almost obsolete by *freehubs*.

G

Gear inches Method of measuring the size of a gear ratio. **See page 135.**

Glycogen A readily available energy source. Carbohydrate is stored as glycogen in your liver and muscles.

Groupset The gear shifters, derailleurs, cassette, hubs, brakes, brake levers and sometimes the chainrings and cranks.

H

Head fairing
An aerodynamic 'helmet' which reduces drag but offers little protection.

High pressure tyre
Also known as a wire on. A high pressure tyre features a wire bead in the casing, which fits beneath a lip running around the inside of the rim. The pressure of the inflated tyre keeps the bead, and hence the tyre, in place.

Honking Standing on the pedals and hauling on the handlebars to increase pedalling power – when riding up hill for instance.

Hub flange The shoulder of the hub, where the holes for the spokes are located.

Hub gear Internal gearing mechanism. Requires little maintenance and is user-friendly. Hub gears are hampered by a limited number and range of gear ratios.

I

Index gearing Click-up, click-down gearing. More user-friendly than friction gearing, where the rider has to feel for each gear.

L

Lactic acid Produced during anaerobic exercise, lactic acid gives a burning feeling in your muscles and prevents them contracting.

Low rider A pannier rack which holds the panniers low down around the axle of the front wheel, giving better balance.

Lugs Pre-cut metal joints into which tubes are brazed during frame making.

M

Maximum heart rate
The highest level at which a cyclist can sustain aerobic exercise. A rule of thumb method of finding it is to subtract your age from 220.

Mech
Slang for derailleur.

N

Nipple
On a spoke, the nipple is a threaded collar that screws onto the spoke on the inner side of the rim. Turning the nipple tightens or loosens the spoke by drawing more

or less of it through the rim. On a cable, the nipple is the soldered-on lump at the end which fits into the gear or brake lever.

P

Peloton French word for the **bunch**. Occasionally spelt peleton.

R

Rake Also known as fork offset, rake is the distance which the fork end is bent forward. It is the distance between a line drawn through the steerer tube and a parallel line drawn through the front drop outs. It has a large effect on *trail*.

Recumbent Bicycle on which the rider sits in a reclined fashion, with the feet out in front. Potentially faster and more comfortable than a conventional bike.

Rolling resistance
Friction of the tyres on the road and the bearings in the wheel hubs. A hard smooth tyre minimizes the tyre's rolling resistance; interestingly, if it's pumped up hard enough the width of the tyre is relatively unimportant.

S

Spider The spider-shaped (or spider-with-legs-missing-shaped) end of the right-hand **crank**.

Spinning Riding with a high **cadence.**

Sprocket A cog on the rear wheel.

Stage race A massed start road race which takes place over several days, with different routes each day.

Steerer tube
Threaded upper end of the front fork, which goes inside the head tube.

Stem Clamped bar shaped like a number seven, which joins the *steerer tube* and the handlebars.

T

TIG welding Short for tungsten inert gas welding. TIG welding melts two tubes directly together, without a joining material.

Time trial An event in which individual cyclists race against the clock over a set distance.

Torque A measure of twisting force. Torque wrenches allow accurate tightening of bolts.

Trail Trail is the distance by which the contact patch of the tyre on the ground trails behind a line drawn through the steering axis (the steerer tube). More trail encourages the front wheel to right itself and point forward; less trail makes sudden tight turns possible, but makes the handling of the bike more 'twitchy'. A Harley Davidson chopper has lots of trail!

Tri bars Clamp on bars, also known as aero bars, that enable a cyclist to adopt a skier's tuck position, greatly reducing *aerodynamic drag*.

Tubular tyre Tyre which totally encases the inner tube, and is glued to the surface of a shallower rim. Traditional road and track racer's tyre.

Turbo trainer
Stationary exercise device which holds the rear wheel of the bike off the floor. The rear wheel drives a weighted fan or a weighted magnet, so that it becomes progressively harder to pedal, simulating the increased effort of cycling on the open road.

Y

Yellow jersey Cycling's ultimate accolade, the yellow jersey is awarded to the Tour de France rider with the lowest cumulative time.

INDEX

PHOTOGRAPHIC ACKNOWLEDGEMENTS

Jacket: All photography by Tim Woodcock, with the exception of the front & back cover centre and front cover bottom right pictures which were supplied by Robert Harding Picture Library

All inside pictures by Tim Woodcock with the exception of the following:
Allsport /Simon Bruty 91 top, /Michael King 94/95, /Mike Powell 88 inset, 89, 96 bottom left, /Pascal Rondeau 86/87, /Jamie Squire 88/89, /Matthew Stockman 4/5, 90/91, /Anton Want 92/93; Francis Cooke 66/67; Hulton Getty Picture Collection 8, 13 top, 132 bottom; Carlton Reid 74 left,

74/75; Stockfile /Steven Behr 78/79, 80 left, 81 right, 84/85, /Dave Stewart 78 left; 178/179.